www.wadsworth.com

wadsworth.com is the World Wide Web site for Wadsworth and is your direct source to dozens of online resources.

At *wadsworth.com* you can find out about supplements, demonstration software, and student resources. You can also send email to many of our authors and preview new publications and exciting new technologies.

wadsworth.com
Changing the way the world learns®

THE WADSWORTH SERIES IN CRIMINOLOGICAL THEORY

2001

Bohm: A Primer on Crime and Delinquency, Second Edition

Fishbein: Biobehavioral Perspectives in Criminology

Messner/Rosenfeld: Crime and the American Dream, Third Edition

Piquero/Mazerolle: Life-Course Criminology: Contemporary and Classic Readings

BIOBEHAVIORAL PERSPECTIVES IN CRIMINOLOGY

DIANA FISHBEIN

Transdisciplinary Behavioral Science Program
Research Triangle Institute

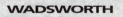

WADSWORTH

THOMSON LEARNING

Australia • Canada • Mexico • Singapore • Spain
United Kingdom • United States

WADSWORTH

★ ™

THOMSON LEARNING

Executive Editor: Sabra Horne
Assistant Editor: Ann Tsai
Developmental Editor: Teri Edwards
Editorial Assistant: Courtney Bruggink
Marketing Manager: Jennifer Somerville
Marketing Assistant: Karyl Davis
Signing Representative: Claire Lynch
Project Editor: Dianne Jensis Toop
Print Buyer: Karen Hunt
Associate Permissions Editor: Stephanie Keough

Production Service: Shepherd Incorporated
Copy Editor: Francine Banworth
Cover Designer: Yvo Riezebos Design
Cover Printer: Webcom Limited
Compositor: Shepherd Incorporated
Printer: Webcom Limited

Library of Congress Cataloging-in-Publication Data

Fishbein, Diana H., 1954–
  Biobehavioral perspectives in criminology /
Diana Fishbein.
    p. cm.
  Includes index.
  ISBN 0-534-54742-7
    1. Criminal behavior—Physiological aspects.
2. Criminal behavior—Genetic aspects. I. Title.
  HV6035.F57 2000
  364.3—dc21   00-043732

Wadsworth/Thomson Learning
10 Davis Drive
Belmont, CA 94002-3098
USA

For more information about our products, contact us:
Thomson Learning Academic Resource Center
1-800-423-0563
http://www.wadsworth.com

International Headquarters
Thomson Learning
International Division
290 Harbor Drive, 2nd Floor
Stamford, CT 06902-7477
USA

UK/Europe/Middle East/South Africa
Thomson Learning
Berkshire House
168-173 High Holborn
London WC1V 7AA
United Kingdom

Asia
Thomson Learning
60 Albert Street, #15-01
Albert Complex
Singapore 189969

Canada
Nelson Thomson Learning
1120 Birchmount Road
Toronto, Ontario M1K 5G4
Canada

Contents

Chapter 4

Biobehavioral Research: Brain Chemistry and Function   35

Chapter 5

Socio-Environmental Contexts   63

Chapter 6

The Negatives: Shortcomings and Controversies   79

Chapter 7

Practical and Policy Implications   **97**

Preface

In the past ten years, biobehavioral sciences research has exploded and substantially enhanced our understanding of human behavior in general. Research findings are particularly relevant to the field of criminology by exposing relationships between genetic, biological, psychological, social, and cultural factors that may eventually help to explain antisocial behavior. This body of research also is beginning to demonstrate ways in which environmental conditions influence behavioral outcomes. Findings suggest that vulnerability to antisocial behavior is partially a function of genetic and biological make-up that is expressed during childhood as particular behavioral, cognitive, and psychological traits. These traits can be measured in physiological and biochemical responses to environmental input. We should not conclude from these findings, however, that distinct genetic and biological factors contribute independently to social dysfunction. Instead, the evidence suggests that a multitude of factors, from the genetic to the social, interact in a constantly evolving and changing dynamic throughout an individual's life. This text provides a comprehensive update of the literature pertinent to criminology and recommends ways in which criminologists can collaborate with other behavioral scientists for an integrated research approach.

The goal of this text is to familiarize students, instructors, researchers, and practitioners with this constantly evolving and rapidly expanding body of research highly relevant to inquiries in the field of criminology. Given that this research base is so vast and includes so many different disciplines, it is impossible for this text to provide a full overview. Instead, specific studies and their findings were selected in an effort to include a variety of perspectives, spanning from the evolutionary and molecular genetic to the psychological and environmental. Some areas of inquiry were left out, not due to their insignificance or lack of research, but due to space limitations (for example, sex offending). Because providing only a selected number of studies and perspectives increases the risk for the appearance of bias, I feel compelled to divulge my biases so that each reader can develop their own informed opinion upon completion of this text.

As an undergraduate, I opted to focus my studies in the field of criminology with a particular interest in etiology—causes—of criminal behavior. Because I was raised in a "criminogenic" neighborhood outside of Washington, D.C., I longed to know why people reared under similar environmental, familial, and social conditions could be so different in level of criminal involvement, and in personality and behavior, from one another. Why, for example, did I not succumb to a life of crime or alcoholism while so many of those I grew up with did? I had hoped my studies in criminology would eventually shed light on these sorts of questions. However, by my junior year in college, what I had learned only reinforced the notion that under similar circumstances, people living in the same environment should all be pretty much alike. It was that year that I discovered other fields in the behavioral sciences, initially from my criminology professor C. Ray Jeffery, and subsequently in a graduate psychobiology program and neuroscience postdoctoral fellowship, where I found promise for eventual answers. Findings from genetics, developmental psychology, behavioral biology, and so forth touched on individual differences in *responses* to similar circumstances; this perspective seemed to be more tangible and less abstract than what was offered by the social sciences alone. My conclusion: the biobehavioral and the social sciences must merge to provide answers and future directions for research and practice.

I did not forget my roots during this transformation, though. In fact, to a great extent, my concerns with prejudice, inequality, child abuse, dissolution of social programs, and neighborhoods allowed by governments to deteriorate were further reinforced by my inquiries. It seemed so obvious to me that while individuals each respond differently to similar social conditions, the presence of an adverse social and physical environment increases risk dramatically for behavioral disorders—not irrespective or in spite of innate predispositions, but in an insidious combination with them. Scientific findings in the biobehavioral sciences support this perspective and I believe now more than ever that social programs are absolutely necessary to provide insulation, strengthen protective factors, reduce effects of risks, and redirect behavioral outcomes. It is important, therefore, that readers recognize the critical role of both the environment and biology in constructing crime prevention and treatment strategies.

With these "biases" in mind, this text attempts to walk the reader through the science of antisocial behavior, beginning with its theoretical and conceptual underpinnings, and through the biobehavioral body of literature that pertains specifically to antisocial behaviors. Many students in criminology do not have a great deal of prior knowledge in genetics and biology. Thus, an attempt is made to make your reading as painless, but informative, as possible! Concepts and terms are described in sufficient detail to familiarize the reader with a scientific area before discussion of findings ensue. Interpretations of the research are qualified so that, once again, the reader can come to his or her own conclusions. Ample discussion is included of the interplay between nature and nurture—biology and social learning—to avoid simplistic and overly confident or causal interpretations. And all of this is framed within the context of topics that interest criminologists.

The text is divided into chapters in a logical way, so that the reader is slowly introduced to the biobehavioral sciences by beginning with an historical context, a theoretical framework, conceptual definitions, and parameters for ongoing studies. Afterwards, more detailed discussions of the biobehavioral sciences are presented followed by a critique of the design and methods, an overview of controversies, and then practical applications. Specifically, then, in the first chapter, the introduction includes an assessment of what the biobehavioral sciences can contribute to the field of criminology. The challenges, controversies, parameters, and limitations of this research base are mentioned with an overview of some of the major works in the field. In addition, an overview of the respective roles of biology and the environment is provided. The second chapter provides a theoretical framework, definitions of concepts, and an integrated model for understanding how all these various related theories can merge to form a more complete understanding of antisocial behavior. Chapter 3 begins the scientific discourse with a description of evolutionary and genetic factors that may play a role in antisocial proclivities. Attention is paid to the controversial nature of evolutionary theories, particularly involving the inability to directly test them. Nevertheless, these theories are considered viable and relevant to human behavior to some extent within the fields of sociobiology and ethology. Genetic research, on the other hand, is imminently more tangible and tremendous advances have been made in understanding disease processes, mental illness, and behavioral disorders with this ever-growing knowledge. An emphasis is placed, however, on interactions between genetic factors and environmental conditions; that is, genes do not "cause" behavior. The fourth chapter is devoted to a presentation of evidence pertaining to antisocial behavior generated by studies of brain chemistry, physiological indicators of arousal and attention, neuropsychological or cognitive function, and neuroimaging techniques. Importantly, this chapter concludes with a substantial section on developmental processes that influence all of these biological factors, in addition to human responses to our environment. In other words, throughout an individual's lifetime, the significance of various biological and environmental influences changes at different stages in life and produces differing effects, depending upon the life stage. These developmental influences are of the utmost importance in understanding behavior, and identifying critical phases at which to intervene. Furthermore, the study of developmental processes demands consideration of interacting biological and environmental factors, bringing to our attention the critical contributions of both. Chapter 5 flows logically from this discussion by highlighting environmental influences on brain function and, in turn, behavior. Contemporary research is increasingly finding that our physical and social environment can alter the way our brains and bodies function in significant ways. Chapter 6 delineates "the negatives"—limitations of the research in terms of methods and interpretations, and political and social controversies that have surrounded the biobehavioral sciences for many years. Although the rigor of this work has increased exponentially in recent years for many reasons, it is still necessary for the reader to be able to identify potential shortcomings in the reports he or she reviews. Similarly, while the controversies have lessened over the years, the absence of criticism, and even some healthy skepticism, will more likely lead to abuses of this body of work. And finally, Chapter 7 discusses practical and policy implications of this work. It is perhaps in this chapter when the reader will begin to identify ways in which this research can be applied, with appropriate caution, to the prevention and treatment of behavioral disorders *and* pathological environments.

COMMENTS TO INSTRUCTORS

This text is, in part, designed to supplement theory books that often provide insufficient detail or overlook this research perspective. A thorough overview of the biobehavioral sciences that relates to criminological inquiries is provided so that instructors do not need to assign a multitude of articles or many different reference materials to cover this topic. It is also unnecessary to rely on sections within existing theory textbooks, which tend to truncate or even neglect this area entirely. As a teaching tool, this is the only text available to inform students and stimulate discussion about biological perspectives without detracting from the materials used routinely in your classrooms. This text is also specifically designed to facilitate studying for comprehensive exams, writing term papers, and to provide a foundation for designing theses or dissertations. Importantly, the materials provided by this text do not conflict with traditional or modern criminological theories—they are presented in such a way as to elaborate and expand upon existing theories. And, throughout the text, you will find qualifications and critiques so that students are able to objectively judge and potentially incorporate this research into their own scholarly thinking with confidence.

ACKNOWLEDGMENTS

I am grateful for the invaluable substantive and editorial comments of David Rowe, Alex Piquero, Deanna Perez, and Christine DeStefano.

INTRODUCTION

Over the past ten years, there has been an explosion of research in the behavioral sciences with direct implications for the study of criminology. Only a decade ago, an article was published in *Criminology* (Fishbein, 1990) that outlined a conceptual framework to incorporate research methodologies and findings generated by various disciplines within the behavioral sciences into the field of criminology. Since then, the methods have increased dramatically in their rigor and reliability, and results of this research have made tremendous strides toward providing a more integrated perspective in our field. For the first time in the history of the behavioral sciences, possibilities for understanding linkages and interactions between genetic, biological, physiological, psychological, social, environmental, and economic factors are in sight. There is speculation that in another ten years, we will have a more complete knowledge of factors that contribute to the developmental pathways that characterize various forms of antisocial behavior (Neihoff, 1999).

Many challenges remain, however, in conducting integrated research that focuses on crime, delinquency, drug abuse, and violence. From a scientific perspective, it is necessary to become familiar with a diverse number of disciplines, some of which use highly technical and field-specific language and technologies. No unified theory or model has emerged as of yet to facilitate our understanding of these fields without having to learn new languages or start anew as undergraduates registered in many different departments. Even more important, no model has been proposed that ties together the perspectives, theories, concepts, terms, and methods of the many disciplines that must be included to conduct truly integrated research. The relative isolation of these various behavioral sciences is unfortunate in light of widespread recognition that the only way to eventually stimulate a comprehensive and accurate understanding of antisocial behavior is through the integration of various disciplines.

The many controversies that surround integrated scientific inquiry have alienated one discipline from another. There is fear that research into genetic contributions to behavior will undermine our conception of free will and will foster the idea that all behavior is due to biological factors. Even more disturbing is the belief that the study of behavioral genetics is inherently racist and may reinforce racial stereotypes, prejudice, and discriminatory practices by the criminal justice system and society-at-large. Furthermore, there are arguments that identification of genetic factors in antisocial behavior will lead to the elimination or low priority of social programs; there may be an attitude of futility that if the problem is genetic, then it must be untreatable or unavoidable. Or worse yet, according to opponents, we may increase reliance on pharmaceutical solutions or futuristic genetic engineering techniques to eliminate the problem of crime, drug abuse, and violence.

These scientific, moral, and social issues are discussed in depth within this text. And while no sure-fire solution is proposed, some direction is given for eventual synthesis of the behavioral sciences as they relate to the study of crime. This text promotes the idea that, with greater familiarity and understanding of the biobehavioral sciences, many fears will be allayed and safeguards can be put into motion. Moreover, increased attention to these issues will lead to informed scrutiny and input from investigators, practitioners, and policy-makers, enhancing potential for both ethical and effective applications of the research findings.

BACK TO THE FUTURE: AN INTEGRATED SCIENCE

Numerous behavioral science subdisciplines, including molecular and behavioral genetics, neurobiology, physiology, psychology, cognitive neuroscience, endocrinology, and forensic psychiatry, provide substantial evidence that certain characteristics of individuals contribute to various traits that increase risk for antisocial behavior. The vast range of studies from these disciplines on vulnerability to antisocial personality disorder, violence, and drug abuse may seem overwhelming at first, but several consistencies across studies reveal a pattern that may characterize vulnerable individuals. Findings indicate that vulnerability to antisocial behavior is partially a function of genetic and biological makeup which is expressed during childhood as particular behavioral, cognitive, and psychological traits, such as impulsivity, attention deficits, aggressiveness, and conduct disorder. These traits have been associated with physiological and biochemical responses to environmental input; for example, heart rate, hormone levels, and EEG recordings are reportedly different in antisocial populations (Raine, 1993). These various biological differences, however, do not function in a vacuum to increase risk. Instead, these factors interact with a multitude of social and environmental conditions in a constantly evolving and changing dynamic to contribute to or protect from social dysfunction. In other words, basic genetic or acquired biological traits are thought to contribute to biochemical and physiological conditions which may predispose individuals to a combination of particular behavioral and psychological outcomes that may occur, or be suppressed, in various environmental settings.

Specifically, evidence is mounting to suggest that several brain chemical systems may be involved in sensation-seeking, impulsivity, negative temperament, and other cognitive and behavioral correlates of antisocial behavior. These chemicals perform somewhat differently between individuals as a result of both genetic factors and social experiences. The particular way they function in an individual determines the level of activity within areas of the brain that are responsible for motivation, emotion, and experiences of pleasure and pain. Although there is a wide range of variation in brain function that is considered normal, the variation itself contributes to personality and temperamental differences between people. Some of these "normal" traits can be associated with either prosocial or antisocial behavior, depending on environmental conditions. For example, the trait sensation-seeking can be related to highly effective practices in the corporate or sports worlds or, conversely, to drug abuse, depending on what sort of environment the individual was raised in (see Figure 1–1).

On the other hand, when certain aspects of brain function occur outside the normal range, behavior and moods can become quite unusual and may be considered "pathological" in extreme cases. Deviations in brain function can be measured in physiological and biochemical processes that influence the behavioral and psychological outcomes. These biological factors are, in turn, influenced by socio-environmental factors which can either contribute to the expression or inhibition of antisocial behaviors. In the presence of negative socio-environmental conditions, like poverty or poor parenting, antisocial behavior becomes more likely. Called *stressors,* these negative conditions act as triggers, offering one explanation for the disproportionate number of residents prone to antisocial behavior in lower income neighborhoods where triggers are more prevalent (Moffitt, 1997). Put simply, abnormalities in certain aspects of brain function can heighten sensitivity to negative environmental circumstances, increasing the risk for an antisocial outcome.

The resulting integration of research findings from various disciplines has direct implications for the study of crime and criminal behavior by providing a scientific foundation for philosophical viewpoints, which should appeal to social scientists who hold widely divergent views and beliefs. This research compels the reader to acknowledge several decades of serious scientific criminological research in psychology, psychiatry, and the biobehavioral sciences. Findings account for both intrapsychic and extra-psychic variables in their emphasis on the recent explosion of genetic and biological evidence that certain aspects of brain function may underlie violent and impulsive behaviors by sensitizing the actor to adverse social stimuli (Pallone & Hennessy, 1996).

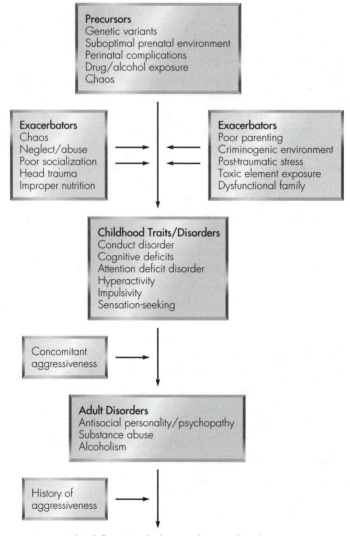

Precursors
Genetic variants
Suboptimal prenatal environment
Perinatal complications
Drug/alcohol exposure
Chaos

Exacerbators
Chaos
Neglect/abuse
Poor socialization
Head trauma
Improper nutrition

Exacerbators
Poor parenting
Criminogenic environment
Post-traumatic stress
Toxic element exposure
Dysfunctional family

Childhood Traits/Disorders
Conduct disorder
Cognitive deficits
Attention deficit disorder
Hyperactivity
Impulsivity
Sensation-seeking

Concomitant
aggressiveness

Adult Disorders
Antisocial personality/psychopathy
Substance abuse
Alcoholism

History of
aggressiveness

Increased Risk for Comorbid Drug Abuse and Violence

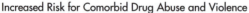

FIGURE 1–1

Drug Abuse and Violence Nexus. Individual Level Risk Factors

Drug abuse and violent behavior often co-occur. This model illustrates how several environmental and biological conditions theoretically interact to increase risk for these behavioral problems. Genetic traits interact with the prenatal environment after conception. Disadvantageous genetic and prenatal conditions during these early stages may be further exacerbated when other "high risk" conditions are added to the mix in early childhood (exacerbators). These ingredients contribute to psychological traits and disorders believed to be related to the onset of drug abuse and violence.

Despite this revolution in the behavioral sciences, there remains unfamiliarity with and resistance to interdisciplinary perspectives, and there has been a lack of communication among various branches of investigation.[1] Unfamiliarity with genetic and biological terminology, methodology, and underlying mechanisms, have hindered exchange between social and biological researchers. As a result, there have been only a few attempts to integrate these disciplines for a more comprehensive understanding of the origins of human behavior generally, and antisocial behavior specifically (see Raine et al., 1997a). That often means we are comfortable with only half of the equation: either the social or biological and genetic contributions. More in-depth examination of this important research domain is essential for practitioners, academicians, policy-makers, and social scientists who would greatly benefit from its knowledge (see Raine & Liu, 1998).

Several substantial works published in the past ten years provide contemporary research overviews and integrative perspectives with direct relevance to the field of criminology. In 1993, Adrian Raine published a leading book on this subject entitled *The Psychopathology of Crime: Criminal Behavior as a Clinical Disorder.* In this work, Raine presented an exhaustive overview of research on antisocial behavior, including evolutionary bases for behavior, genetics, neurochemistry, neuropsychology, brain imaging, psychophysiology, and physical and social environmental variables. In a later book, Raine and his colleagues (1997a) assembled over thirty chapters authored by several internationally prominent researchers on the biosocial bases of violence. While they acknowledge that biological research on various types of antisocial behavior is still in short supply, not always clearly enunciated, and rife with conceptual and theoretical issues not yet resolved, they also demonstrate that integrative works are actively in progress, report many consistent findings, and provide direction in terms of factors that are potentially important and fruitful methodological approaches. Other notable texts include those by Volavka (1995) on the neurobiology of violence, The National Research Council (Reiss et al., 1994) on biobehavioral influences on violence, Hillbrand and Pallone (1993) on the psychobiology of aggression, The Ciba Foundation Symposium (Bock & Goode, 1996) on the genetics of criminality, Pallone and Hennessy (1996) on contemporary interdisciplinary perspectives in the study of aggression, and Fishbein and Pease on both the social, environmental, genetic, and biological engines in drug abuse (1996) and on the science, treatment, and prevention of antisocial behavior (1999). Evolutionary theories of crime have been thoroughly reviewed by Daly (1996) and Ellis and Walsh (1997).

---

[1]Unfamiliarity with biobehavioral findings and methods has also bred suspicions of consequent racism, stigmatization, and oppressive treatments (see Proceedings of the Genetics and Crime Conference in 1995, sponsored by the University of Maryland and the Human Genome Project, NIH).

Numerous other works have also substantially furthered progress in interdisciplinary research on antisocial behavior (e.g., Bardo et al., 1996; Glantz & Pickens, 1991; Lappalainen et al., 1998; Moffitt et al., 1989; O'Connor et al., 1998a; Piquero & Tibbetts, 1999; Rowe et al., 1998a, 1998b; Tarter & Vanyukov, 1994; Virkkunen et al., 1996). Interestingly, several of these works have been produced by drug abuse researchers who have provided significant guidance with respect to possible underlying mechanisms in behavioral problems, environmental interactions, and models for comprehensive studies. Drug abuse and addiction are strongly correlated with and oftentimes preceded by antisocial behaviors, including conduct disorder, antisocial personality disorder, attention deficit hyperactivity disorder, impulsive-aggressiveness, and many other psychological and temperamental characteristics. Findings from drug abuse studies suggest that drug abuse and antisocial behaviors share many antecedent conditions and may arise from similar biological and social engines (see Fishbein, 1998 for review). This research has been instrumental in identifying aspects of brain function and environmental triggers that may relate to various antisocial behaviors that warrant further investigation.

In spite of this progress, several limitations in the research remain. For one, many so-called "interdisciplinary" works tend to focus on biological factors and, rather than attempt to estimate relative influences, simply control for social variables. Also, many studies do not account for ongoing environmental influences on biological conditions, treating them as if they were fixed and uncorrectable. Furthermore, this body of research has yet to account for population or groupwide collective aggression and antisocial behavior, nor for the antisocial practices of corporations and political bodies. These shortfalls, among many others (described in Chapter 6), could be addressed by the behavioral sciences in more meaningful ways by incorporating the perspectives and methodologies of social scientists.

The purpose of this supplementary text is to define concepts and terms and to present a model for interdisciplinary investigation in the field of criminology (see Fishbein, 1990; Tarter & Vanyukov, 1994; Barratt & Slaughter, 1998). A summary of contemporary biobehavioral research findings are presented for students and scholars in criminology who wish to familiarize themselves with the developmental pathway of the research itself. Findings are reported which pertain to behavioral phenotypes (the observable and measurable behavioral results of the interaction between genes and environment) which constitute the various dimensions of antisocial behavior, for example, impulsivity, aggressiveness, substance abuse, childhood behavioral disorders, and attention deficits (not included are studies on sex offending, instrumental aggression, and several other aspects of deviance). This area of research is moving quickly and is funded by agencies largely external to the U.S. Department of Justice and other sources more familiar to the criminologist or criminal justice professional. It is critical that we, as criminologists and practitioners, maintain a familiarity with this research so that it does not escape our scrutiny and input.

In the next chapter, definitions and concepts for this area of study are presented, and a theoretical model for understanding the relationship between genes and the environment is introduced. In Chapter 3, pertinent literature from the behavioral sciences is summarized, including evolutionary theories, and behavioral and molecular genetics. Chapter 4 discusses biochemistry (neurotransmitters and hormones), physiology (electrophysiological measures, skin conductance, and heart rate), neuropsychology and imaging research, and developmental psychology. Chapter 5 highlights environmental influences on brain function that increase risk for antisocial behavior. In Chapter 6, methodological shortcomings of this research are presented and suggestions for improving research designs and instruments are made. Chapter 6 also identifies issues that arise from a study of underlying genetic and biological factors in antisocial behavior and produce significant controversy in the field. And finally, Chapter 7 discusses practical and policy implications and limitations of current research findings.

THEORETICAL FRAMEWORK, DEFINITIONS, AND CONCEPTS

Theories in criminology have not traditionally included genetic or biological factors. For this reason, it is important that a model is developed to show how genetic and biological conditions presumably interact with social, environmental, and psychological factors to influence risk for antisocial behaviors. In order to create this framework or model for incorporating biological perspectives into criminological theory, we must first identify the sorts of behaviors that are relevant to study. This exercise is essential given that not all "illegal" behaviors are harmful or antisocial and not all "legitimate" behaviors are moral, acceptable, or adaptive. Thus, a distinction between criminality and antisocial behavior must be drawn so that behaviors to be included in this model can be isolated and studied.

CRIMINALITY VERSUS ANTISOCIAL BEHAVIOR

Criminal and antisocial behavior overlap in obvious ways, but are distinct in ways that are not always apparent. The term *criminality* includes behaviors that do not necessarily offend all members of society, such as certain "victimless" acts that appear to affect only the person who engages in that behavior, example given, loitering and some forms of illicit drug use. Criminality also includes behaviors that may be considered adaptive or rational given the social conditions and circumstances. For example, in a deprived environment, it may be considered rational for an individual to steal in order to obtain food or shelter. Aggressive behaviors are also adaptive in many circumstances and only when the aggression is extreme, unprovoked, and out-of-context in that particular setting can aggression be considered maladaptive. In these cases, the aggression is usually also "criminalized" by the system. The concept of criminality also excludes behaviors that may be antisocial or illegal but that are not detected by the criminal justice system (CJS). In other words, it is necessary for an individual who committed an illegal behavior to be caught, charged, and convicted by the CJS to earn the label "criminal."

Antisocial behaviors, on the other hand, are costly or injurious to the individual perpetrator, other citizens, and/or society overall. Such behaviors do not necessarily violate legal norms or come to official attention, however. Antisocial individuals have a high probability of being labeled (i.e., charged and convicted) as delinquent or criminal, but being labeled as such is not sufficient to be identified as antisocial. An example of individuals who may behave in an antisocial way include schizophrenics. The behavior of schizophrenics tends to be poorly regulated, detrimental to their own wellbeing, and considered "deviant," but they rarely engage in crime. Nevertheless, definitive research has established that biochemical factors contribute substantially to this disorder and they must be addressed in a potentially effective treatment strategy. Individuals identified as psychopathic (see Chapter 3), on the other hand, are at high risk for crime by virtue of their behavior. Yet, there are psychopathic individuals who find legal, albeit not always ethical, avenues for channeling their behavioral tendencies (e.g., a subgroup of those involved in competitive sports, high risk activities, corporate life, and politics). The focus of this book is on antisocial behaviors, including both criminal and undetected deviant behaviors, that are detrimental to the individuals affected and/or their milieu; in other words, behaviors that increase the risk that an individual will be labeled a "criminal," for example, violence or drug abuse.

Criminal Behavior	Antisocial Behavior
Not necessarily offensive to most people	Offends most people
Includes victimless crimes	Usually excludes victimless crimes
Depends on detection by the criminal justice system or defined as criminal from self-reported surveys	At risk for criminal behavior, but does not depend on detection by criminal justice system
Can be either poor regulated or an adaptive strategy given the environment	Poor regulated and detrimental to self and/or others
Violates criminal laws	Does not necessarily violate criminal laws
Criminal	Deviant

It should also be understood that this area of scientific inquiry focuses upon the behaviors and traits that precede antisocial behavior. We are not only interested in the types of behaviors that get people into trouble in their adulthood; it is also important to identify the psychological, temperamental, and behavioral traits that develop into larger problems as the individual ages. That is why it is important to study Attention Deficit/Hyperactivity Disorder, Conduct Disorder, early childhood aggression, and other traits that are known to occur earlier in an individual's life and are predictive of later more serious problems. Thus, antisocial behavior manifests itself differently, depending on the particular age the person is in during the life course; two-year-olds are not likely to get arrested and convicted for assault. But they have been known to hit people and hurt animals. Children who do a lot of this are more likely to be increasingly antisocial as they age, and potentially become labeled as "criminals" by our CJS.

Multiple Dimensions of Antisocial Behavior

Studies generated from this perspective in criminology focus on the various dimensions of antisocial behavior that can be more reliably and precisely measured than criminal behavior. Antisocial behavior is not a unitary phenomenon; there are many different aspects that need to be studied separately and interactively. Dimensions of antisocial behavior can be both behavioral and psychological traits, including excessive aggression, hostility or negative affect, compulsions and other excessive tendencies, drug abuse, inability to experience remorse or empathy, insensitivity to consequences, among many others. Other than excessive aggression, which by definition involves injury to others, none of these other behavioral and personality traits are inherently antisocial. When they are coupled with a lack of regard for consequences or for other individuals, however, the behavioral pattern can be characterized as antisocial. Thus, the presence of these features operates by increasing the risk for antisocial behavior. When several of these traits exist in the same individual, the risk increases substantially.

By dissecting the dimensions of antisocial behavior that are to be studied, the researcher is, in essence, isolating the *behavioral phenotypes* that correlate or co-occur with criminal behavior. A phenotype is the result of the continuous interaction between genetic factors and environmental experiences. For example, even something as simple as eye color is a result of both genetic influence and the environment during pregnancy. Behavioral phenotypes are much more complex than appearance, but can still be observed, measured, and manipulated. Thus, they are imminently better candidates for investigation than criminality, which is a socially constructed concept. Phenotypes of interest to the criminologist, which correlate or co-occur with criminal behavior, include aggressiveness, impulsivity, attention and other cognitive deficits, hyperactivity, and negative affect.

Studies need to specify the particular dimension(s) being focused on so that investigators can more accurately and consistently define the sort of antisocial behavior of interest. One problem that exists throughout the behavioral sciences is the lack of specification or the use of different measurement tools, leading to different and oftentimes conflicting results. Using similar concepts and definitions instead, investigators will be able to replicate or find steady support for their findings to eventually identify consistencies among studies and base conclusions on rigorous and reliable methods of measuring behavior.

Characterizing Antisocial Behavior

As a phenomenon to be studied, *antisocial behavior* is a complex concept defined variably in different disciplines and arising from widely diverging origins. No single mental disorder is uniquely associated with antisocial behavior, nor are particular behavioral patterns, childhood experiences, or social circumstances. Even though there are many ways to characterize these individuals, there appears to be a subgroup of offenders that is known to persistently engage in impulsive (not instrumental) antisocial behavior (see e.g., Nagin & Farrington, 1992). Their behavior is potentially violent (resulting in physical injury) and is not simply understood by knowing the behavioral outcome. Instead, they can be characterized by relatively stable personality and temperamental traits, including impulsivity, negative affect, and cognitive deficits. Displays of impulsive antisocial behavior are, then, an outgrowth of these traits in interaction with crime-prone situations in the social environment. Conversely, individuals who exhibit only single displays of antisocial behavior may be more influenced by social and situational factors and probably do not possess the necessary conditions to produce a true "vulnerability" to a destructive behavioral pattern. This description corresponds with the pattern described by Moffitt (1993), who characterizes a subgroup of chronic offenders by "life-course persistent antisocial behavior culminating in a pathologic personality." Individuals possessing these features also appear to be unusually susceptible to the abuse of alcohol or drugs.

Due to the nature of the phenomenon of antisocial behavior, research to understand the origins and underlying mechanisms in criminal behavior must focus on the measurable dimensions (phenotypes) of antisocial behavior that may increase the risk for criminal activity. A focus on crime, per se, is misguided from a measurement standpoint since crime is an abstract legal and social construct, not a measurable behavioral construct. Criminal acts that are committed only once or rarely by an individual may be more a result of a situation than an ongoing predisposition. But a longstanding or recurrent pattern of antisocial behavior is more likely due to the cumulative, developmental influence of interacting biological and environmental factors.

A THEORETICAL MODEL FOR INTEGRATED RESEARCH

The theoretical framework for biobehavioral perspectives in criminology is consistent with the view that all human behavior is the result of the relationship between traits that people enter into the world with and their subsequent experiences in the social and physical world. This perspective is embodied in the *diathesis-stress model,* created to describe factors that may contribute to many forms of antisocial behavior. According to this model, individuals vary considerably with respect to their biological strengths and weaknesses. Biological and genetic weaknesses are referred to as a "vulnerability" or disadvantage and can include traits that people are born with or that develop in response to their environment. These vulnerabilities influence the degree to which the individual is at risk for antisocial behavior. Rather than acting alone, however, these biological features operate by setting the stage for how adaptively an individual will respond to stressful experiences. In other words, a stressful environment is more likely to contribute to some form of behavioral or psychological problem when the individual experiencing it possesses a biological system that is somehow compromised. Learning disability, brain damage or functional irregularity, drug exposure, genetic predisposition to temperamental disturbances, and other biological disadvantages lay the groundwork for a pathological response to stress. Learning experiences contribute further by either increasing or decreasing the risk.

Although the probability of a pathological response is a function of the number of these risk factors present, the probability is even greater in the presence of an adverse environment with severe stressors (e.g., poverty, unemployment, crime and drug infestation, poor parenting, lack of education, abuse/ neglect, social immobility). For example, hyperactive children may function well given appropriate intervention. In the presence of family instability, alcoholism, absence of educational programs, and a delinquent peer group, however, the child may be more prone to antisocial behavior, possibly resulting in criminal acts. Thus, environmental factors can lead to the expression of antisocial behavior in vulnerable persons. Environmental factors may be even more influential in contributing to antisocial behavior than strictly biological vulnerabilities when the environment is unusually harsh or conducive to such behavior, as we may readily observe in some of our inner cities. Once again, however, not all inner-city residents engage in antisocial behavior; that outcome remains somewhat dependent on individual vulnerability. The reverse may also apply— even in the presence of a protective environment, a biological disadvantage may be so severe as to overwhelm the positive environmental influence. An example of that particular outcome may be seen in fetal alcohol syndrome, when the biological odds of having poorly regulated behavior due to prenatal alcohol exposure frequently outweigh prosocial influences (see Figure 2–1).

EXAMPLES OF NATURE PLUS NURTURE

Investigators no longer believe that human behavior is either due to nature (biological causes) or nurture (social causes) alone. As described by the diathesis stress model, these two conditions interact in a dynamic and fluid way throughout an individual's life. Some examples of the interaction between biology and the social environment in human behavior are presented here.

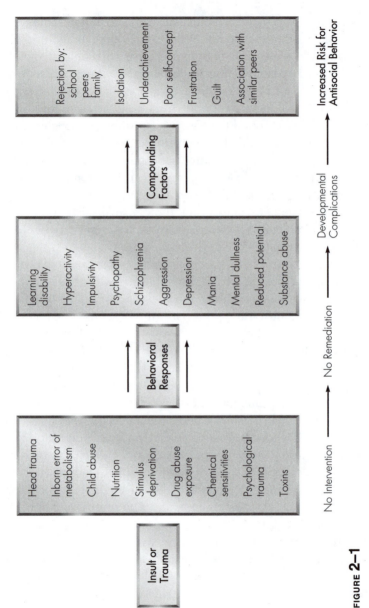

Insult or Trauma

Head trauma
Inborn error of metabolism
Child abuse
Nutrition
Stimulus deprivation
Drug abuse exposure
Chemical sensitivities
Psychological trauma
Toxins

Behavioral Responses

Learning disability
Hyperactivity
Impulsivity
Psychopathy
Schizophrenia
Aggression
Depression
Mania
Mental dullness
Reduced potential
Substance abuse

Compounding Factors

Rejection by:
school
peers
family
Isolation
Underachievement
Poor self-concept
Frustration
Guilt
Association with similar peers

No Intervention → No Remediation → Developmental Complications → **Increased Risk for Antisocial Behavior**

FIGURE 2–1

The Developmental Stages of Antisocial Behavior.

Biochemistry Plus Social Hierarchy

Neurotransmitters, described in more detail in Chapter 3, are chemical messengers in the brain that allow brain cells and regions to communicate with each other. These chemicals are responsible for a variety of brain functions, from eating and drinking patterns, to memory and learning processes, to emotions and moods. Serotonin is a neurotransmitter of particular interest for its role in impulsivity and aggressiveness. Low levels of activity and metabolism of serotonin have been associated with both, which is perhaps the most reliable finding in the history of psychiatry. An individual's range for synthesis and metabolism of serotonin is largely determined by his or her genes, although its activity is exquisitely sensitive to changes in the environment. Animal studies show that, when the social hierarchy is altered, the loss in status by dominant monkeys results in decreases in serotonin activity and vice versa (Edwards & Kravitz, 1997; Higley et al., 1996; Raleigh et al., 1991), and they become more impulsive and aggressive. Human studies consistently report lower levels of serotonin in individuals exposed to high and chronic amounts of stress (e.g., Post-Traumatic Stress Disorder [PTSD]) than individuals not exposed to high levels of stress (Dinan, 1996; Graeff et al., 1996; Petty et al., 1996; Stokes, 1995). Studies further show that poor parenting is associated with low serotonin levels in the child (Pine et al., 1996, 1997) and good parenting techniques may actually raise serotonin activity levels (Field et al., 1998), thereby minimizing the impact of other risk factors for negative behavioral outcomes. These findings in general support the notion that the integrity of serotonin function is directly influenced by environmental factors, most notably the experience of stress, and that alterations in the environment to reduce stress may enhance its function.

Temperament Plus Learning

Temperament is relatively stable across the life span (Plomin & Daniels, 1987) and includes traits such as introversion, shyness, extroversion, depressed mood, elevated or positive mood, risk taking or sensation-seeking, impulsivity, among many others. Temperamental features are known to be largely heritable; in other words, a significant amount of variation in the trait is genetic, which explains why it tends to be so stable and consistent in an individual. Nevertheless, the behavioral expression of any given temperament strongly depends on environmental circumstances, such as stressors, situational factors, opportunities, and learning experiences. Shyness is one form of temperament with biological and genetic origins that can be altered through environmental manipulations to influence its behavioral manifestations. A part of the nervous system which resides outside of the brain itself is called the autonomic nervous system (ANS). It is largely responsible for various functions necessary for our survival, including the regulation of heart rate, blood pressure, digestion, body temperature, circulation and so forth. The ANS is also activated under stressful circumstances; for example, panic attacks are the result of the ANS gone awry. Reasons for this association between stress and ANS activity pertain to survival. ANS activation, by affecting the functions just described, unleashes energy stores in the brain and body and mobilizes an individual for action. An unfortunate side effect, however, is that the experience of stress produces discomfort through its effects on the ANS. Interestingly, individuals who are uncomfortable in unfamiliar social situations have been characterized as having relatively high levels of ANS activity and, as a result, they withdraw to avoid what is perceived as excessive levels of social stimulation (Schmidt & Fox, 1994). Effective strategies to combat shyness by lowering levels of reactivity of the ANS in an individual may result in more extroverted behavior and less nervousness in social situations (Gunnar et al., 1997; Kagan, 1992; Kagan et al., 1988; Schmidt et al., 1997). This can be accomplished by either behavioral modification techniques or medication.

Genetic Liability Plus Family Functioning

Third, alcoholism, thought to be significantly influenced by genes and associated with several genetic markers contributing to its expression, is also susceptible to environmental influence. While alcoholism is considered to be in large part a genetic disease state, its expression is significantly dependent upon family stability factors which may act as buffers or protectors (Finney & Moos, 1992; Hussong & Chassin, 1997; Power & Estaugh, 1990). The same may also be true for other forms of drug abuse and addiction in which genetics plays a role, but the environment and learning experiences help to determine their actual expression.

Neurotoxicity Plus Environmental Enrichment

A significant population of children chronically exposed to cocaine prenatally have been characterized as difficult to manage, temperamental, hyperresponsive to environmental stimuli (e.g., lights and noises), developmentally delayed, learning disabled, impulsive, and sometimes aggressive. Cocaine can dramatically alter the developing nervous system to increase the likelihood of these behaviors in predictable ways (Azuma & Chasnoff, 1993; Brooke-Gunn et al., 1994; Giacoia, 1990; Mayes et al., 1993; Mott et al., 1993). Because the brain continues to develop for at least twelve months after birth, however, the provision of supportive therapies and interventions can substantially alter these negative outcomes. Children raised by the "crack mothers" who gave birth to them exhibit significantly worse behavioral and cognitive outcomes than cocaine-exposed children raised in more supportive and nurturing environments (Hofkosh et al., 1995; Zuckerman & Bresnahan, 1991), suggesting that, although prenatal cocaine exposure is a highly preventable cause of behavioral and cognitive disorders, environmental enrichment during the formative years can substantially improve the outcome (Field et al., 1998).

Cognitive Ability Plus Experience

One final example of the nature-nurture interaction is that of cognitive differences between males and females. Similar to other parts of the anatomy, the structure of the developing fetal brain is influenced after the seventh week of pregnancy by the introduction of testosterone, a male hormone, in fetuses with a Y chromosome—males. Changes in neuroanatomy that result from prenatal exposure to this male hormone cause the male brain to be distinctively different from the female brain, as well as promote the development of external genitalia, a larger musculature and, eventually, facial hair. One result of these differences in neuroanatomy is distinctive styles of thinking (i.e., cognition), with males and females performing somewhat differently in various cognitive tasks. For example, males have been found to be somewhat superior to females on average in spatial skills, while females on average have better verbal ability.

Interestingly, however, the gender gap in these cognitive differences has been narrowing in recent decades. Can the environment produce such significant changes in a trait like cognition which is thought to be largely genetic? Researchers believe that differences in the way parents and society treat their children may contribute to cognitive styles and actually alter brain development in the early years (Bjorklund & Brown, 1998). A few decades ago, psychological studies found that parents were more likely to encourage exploration of the environment and active play in baby boys, while little girls were coddled, comforted, and "kept safe" from their environment. In contrast, parents in more recent years tend to treat male and female babies more equally. Handling boy and girl babies in similar ways may mean an increase in activity levels for baby girls which, in turn, may lead to a smaller magnitude of gender differences in cognitive abilities.

SUMMARY

There are many varieties of theories in the field of criminology, some of which are competitive with each other (e.g., conflict and differential association theories), while others are considered to be "integrated" because they combine several criminological perspectives. The research described in this text does not fall into either of these categories. Biobehavioral research does reflect certain ways of thinking and modeling relationships between variables, but it should not be considered in terms of theories that are competitive with others in criminology. Instead, this text describes a body of research that reflects a broad range of scientific perspectives and research methods used to better understand human behavior, which are highly relevant to the questions posed by criminologists. Findings from the biobehavioral sciences should, therefore, be viewed as having the potential to fill existing gaps in our knowledge relating to the development of antisocial behavior, and to eventually be understood in the context of social forces that we have identified as significant players in this dynamic equation.

There are no exceptions to the assertion that all complex human behavior is the result of interactions between our genes and our environment. Even behaviors that are predominantly learned alter all future behaviors by modifying the way brain cells function and communicate, producing an essential feedback loop of information exchanged between neurological systems and the environment. This process is not, therefore, static or predestined. Throughout the life span, developmental changes reflective of age-related stages and differential experiences occur in a fluid way so that the pathway an individual follows can be altered, inadvertently or intentionally.

The field of criminology has concentrated on theories and concepts that revolve around experiential factors, whether they be systemwide, interpersonal, or individual. They do not, by nature, exclude the influence of genetic and biological conditions; rather, they simply do not provide a model that would accommodate their consideration. Thus, the next step is to discuss the ever-increasing body of biobehavioral research and, subsequently, begin to fit models together to demonstrate their compatibility and complementary dimensions.

BIOBEHAVIORAL RESEARCH: EVOLUTION AND GENETICS

CHAPTER

3

Recent scientific discoveries and technological and informational advancements have potential to move the fields of physical, mental, and public health forward at a rapid pace toward the vision of optimal health for all individuals. In particular, the year 2000 has brought with it an understanding that human behavior is a complex, multidimensional phenomenon with origins rooted in many factors, from the genetic to the environmental. If our goal is to eventually prevent and treat disorders of the body and mind, it is critical that we more fully understand the relationship between genetic and environmental factors. It would be unrealistic to expect investigators to become proficient in all relevant fields. Nevertheless, given the present state of research and development, it is clearly advantageous for there to be an academic environment that supports communication, exchange of ideas, and familiarity with the evidence across disciplines. Thus, new developments and capabilities provide a compelling basis for the creation of "transdisciplinary" programs that bring together relevant fields. There is wide recognition within the scientific elite that next steps in research must necessarily involve eliminating traditional disciplinary boundaries if we are to take advantage of our current growth in knowledge and technology. Specialization within disciplines remains critical; however, specialization must not be equated with the isolation of fields and lack of an integrated conceptual framework for scientific inquiry.

Given the critical interaction between genes and environment in human behavior, the biobehavioral sciences have concentrated on various conditions that both act as protective factors and risk factors in the development of behavioral disorders. A particular interest in crime, violence, and drug abuse leads researchers to focus, in particular, on risk factors that may trigger or cause an underlying tendency toward antisocial behavior. Thus, threaded throughout this review of behavioral sciences research are references to the role of *stress,* believed to play a significant role in human behavioral outcomes and constituting, to a great degree, the environmental part of the equation.

19

Understanding the dynamics and consequences of stress is key to unraveling etiological mechanisms in antisocial outcomes.

As described in depth in Chapter 5, stress is not just the feeling of being overwhelmed by work or having a disagreement with a friend. In basic terms, it is the physical and psychological response to an excess of stimulation compared with an individual's resources for coping (Meaney et al., 1996). Stress comes in different sizes and shapes, but here we refer to the sort of stress that can have lasting effects. Excessive levels of stimulation may come from either social or biological sources, or be due to an interaction of both.

Examples and Sources of Stress

Social	Biological
Child abuse and neglect	Lead or pesticide poisoning
Family dysfunction	Head trauma
Sensory deprivation	Prenatal drug exposure
Observing violence	Thyroid dysfunction
Lack of early bonding	Drug or alcohol intake
Poverty	Chronic physical illness
Racial discrimination	Mental illness

Resources for coping with that stimulation may also be grounded in conditions that are either biological (e.g., IQ and cognitive skills), social (e.g., parenting techniques), psychological (e.g., self-efficacy) or, most likely, a combination. The presence of a long-term or reoccurring stressor often results in a cumulative effect on biological and physiological responses which can impair coping abilities, and becomes a significant risk factor. As a consequence, chronic stress compromises an individual's ability to respond to environmental conditions in an adaptive way, and thus increases the likelihood of psychopathology or antisocial behavior (Anisman & Zacharko, 1986). Inherent susceptibilities or vulnerabilities help to determine particular behavioral outcomes of that stress, example, from schizophrenia to depression to violence, while positive attributes of either the individual or the environment can provide some protection from these outcomes.

The first half of this chapter highlights the role of evolutionary forces in antisocial behavior. Evolution is a controversial concept, and yet it has been instrumental in forming the groundwork for modern biology and, thus, should be included in a comprehensive discussion of the biobehavioral sciences. On the other hand, due to the long time periods involved, evolutionary forces are difficult to isolate and define, measure and manipulate so its effects cannot be directly studied in humans. Thus, the study of these forces has been wrought with difficulties and criticisms. The latter half of this chapter discusses genetics and attempts to simplify some unusually technical concepts and technologies. Even a cursory understanding of genetics, however, will enable the reader to more accurately place *inherent tendencies, genetic traits,* or *predispositions* into context by realizing that genetic factors are neither fixed nor immune to environmental influences.

EVOLUTIONARY DICTATES (ADAPTED FROM ELLIS AND WALSH'S BOOK, *CRIMINOLOGY: A GLOBAL PERSPECTIVE*, 2000)

There is irrefutable evidence from fossil records that all of the types of animals, insects, birds, and other organisms that have existed on earth have dramatically changed over millions of years. Biologists call this record of change *evolution.* Charles Darwin proposed the most widely accepted theory of evolution; his explanations about how and why organisms undergo gradual change throughout many generations were revolutionary. Modern genetics have confirmed, strengthened, and expanded on his theories, leading to the Neo-Darwinian theory of today. At the heart of all versions of Darwin's theory is the idea that species arise and eventually become extinct due to the tendency of individual members within a species to reproduce at different rates, depending on environmental conditions. This is called *natural selection.* Our genes actually dictate that reproduction is the most vital function an organism has; DNA codes for the priority reproduction must take in order for a species to ultimately survive. When individual members of a species either decide not to reproduce or are unable to, their particular combination of genes ceases to exist upon their death. Under conditions which make it difficult for the species as a whole to reproduce, extinction becomes possible. Thus, reproduction is an evolutionary phenomenon that is driven by our genes which code for the design of anatomical and physiological traits, including the brain. This process has important implications for a variety of behaviors that revolve around reproductive drives.

Most evolutionists assume that natural selection, through the activity of many genes, operates as much on behavior as it does on anatomical and physiological traits. Following this assumption, some criminologists have applied Darwinian ideas to the study of criminal behavior. Thinking about criminality in evolutionary terms has led to questions about the reproductive consequences not only for offending, but also for crime control and prevention efforts that develop in response to crime. Perhaps both have at least partly evolved by natural selection.

Evidence that genes contribute to variation in criminal behavior does not prove that evolutionary theory can help in understanding such behavior—the jury is still out. However, if genes are not responsible for significant variation in such behavior, the argument that evolutionary theory could help in understanding criminal behavior would be seriously undercut. Consequently, researchers working from an evolutionary perspective have been keenly interested in the so-called *genetic influence hypothesis,* as discussed later. Several lines of evidence have pointed toward evolutionary-based genetic influences on antisocial behavior. Genetic mechanisms that may be particularly involved in antisocial behavior are detailed in the latter half of this chapter.

Five evolutionary theories that pertain to antisocial behavior have been recently proposed: the cheater theory, the r/K theory, conditional adaptation theory, alternative adaptation theory, and the evolutionary expropriative theory. While all five theories are rooted in the same overarching Neo-Darwinian theory of evolution, each one emphasizes somewhat different features of this overarching theory. Once again, these theories have not been proven or disproven, but they are consistent with what is known about evolutionary processes in general.

Cheater Theory

The cheater theory was inspired by evidence that in several species, some males have evolved what are termed *alternative reproductive strategies;* there are different approaches that males can take to ensure their reproduction. These strategies are made possible by the fact that males do not need to grow (i.e., gestate) offspring in order to reproduce, as do females. This gives males a much higher reproductive capacity than females, which in turn offers them greater latitude than females have in their approaches to their reproductive behavior.

In species that have evolved distinct alternative reproductive strategies, at least two subpopulations of males are found. Among the names given to these subpopulations are "dads" and "cads." Dads reproduce mainly by fulfilling female preferences for males who are able and prone to provide substantial parental care for offspring. Cads, on the other hand, have evolved various methods of using either force or deception in order to mate without providing adequate offspring care.

According to proponents of the cheater theory, persistent criminals are human cads. Proponents of the cheater theory such as Linda Mealey (1995) have contended that some males may simply learn to become cads through social and/or environmental experiences, while others are genetically inclined to approach reproduction in this way. Those who are almost completely genetically programmed to be cheaters and exhibit symptoms early in life are called psychopaths.

To put the cheater theory more formally, females have evolved preferences for males who will provide resources and assistance in rearing offspring. In a number of species, including humans, the genes programming males have responded to this female preference with an alternative reproductive strategy: that of a cheater or cad. Theoretically, cheater males have evolved in human populations just as in several other species, especially in large impersonal societies where it is most difficult for their strategy to be detected by prospective mates. Given their tendency toward deceptive means to obtain mates, these males approach other situations in similar ways—by deception, cheating, theft, risk taking, and other victimful offenses.

r/K Theory

According to r/K theory, individual animals can be placed along a continuum of successful approaches to reproduction, and a number of physical, mental, and behavioral traits coincide in predictable ways with this continuum of strategies. Some species evolve more slowly and, thus, reproduce less frequently, while other species evolve quickly and reproduce in large numbers. Individuals or groups that evolve tendencies to reproduce slowly not only must have fewer offspring, but must spend more time gestating each one and then caring for them more carefully after birth—this is termed the K strategy. Rapidly reproducing organisms, on the other hand, tend to emphasize producing larger numbers of offspring, but without spending as much time gestating and caring for each one—this is called the r strategy.

Those who have applied the r/K concept to the study of criminal behavior have made two assumptions: First, even though humans as a whole are extremely K in their approach to reproduction, there is still some variability among us. Second, victimizing behavior within a species is an expression of a relatively r-approach to reproduction. If so, criminals and antisocial individuals can be thought of as being more prone toward a r strategy than other people.

According to the r/K theory, criminal and antisocial people will tend to have a shorter term in pregnancy, lower birth weights, larger numbers of siblings and offspring, and they will begin engaging in sexual behavior earlier and with more partners than is the case for other people in general. To account for why males are more criminal than females, the theory asserts that males are more prone toward an r-approach with respect to reproduction than females. There is evidence for this theory in that, on average, offenders have a greater history of prenatal and perinatal complications, come from larger families, and engage in sexual behavior earlier and more frequently than nonoffender populations. The main proponents of this theory are Philippe Rushton (1990, 1995) and Lee Ellis (1987, 1989).

Conditional Adaptation Theory

The conditional adaptation theory asserts that antisocial behavior is part of a broad adaptive response to an unstable and hostile environment. The theory's proponents believe that people in general are genetically inclined to begin early in life weighing their environmental options as far as reproduction and survival are concerned. During the first few years of life, children who live in chaotic and hostile environments will begin puberty early, and will complement this early physical development with an early onset of sexual activity. In adulthood, these same individuals will have unstable relationships and will not be very inclined to engage in child rearing. Interestingly, evidence to support this theory exists in findings that show early onset of puberty and early sexual behavior in both male and female delinquents, and unstable relationships and poor parenting techniques in adult criminals relative to the general population.

Conditional adaptation theory asserts that if the same individuals were to be reared in predictable, caring environments, their reproductive development would be delayed, as would the onset of sexual activity. In addition, a stable caring environment would prevent most children from developing the sort of opportunistic approaches to reproduction that incline them to violate criminal statutes. Such an environment is conducive of a lower rate of reproduction and a more evenly evolving population. It also contributes to more stable and altruistic behavioral patterns. The main proponent of conditional adaptation theory is Jay Belsky (1980, 1993, Belsky et al., 1991, 1997).

Alternative Adaptation Theory

According to David Rowe, the primary advocate of alternative adaptation theory, humans are genetically programmed to vary in tendencies to engage in antisocial behavior. In other words, some people have strong antisocial tendencies, some have virtually none, and most are intermediate. This assumption is the opposite of the one made by proponents of the conditional adaptation theory, who assume that mostly all humans have an equal genetic potential for antisocial behavior.

Rowe distinguishes between mating effort and parenting effort, and asserts that those who are most prone to engage in criminal or antisocial behavior have evolved tendencies to emphasize mating effort. In other words, they are more interested in locating prospective mates for sexual purposes than they are in parenting offspring. From these premises, alternative adaptation theory leads to the hypothesis that offenders will more often be males, prone toward sensation-seeking, aggressive, and have a strong sex drive. Intelligence also plays a central role; those with high intelligence will be able to carry out more long-term and socially complex strategies to obtain resources than those with low intelligence. Therefore, those with high intelligence will gravitate toward parenting effort, and those with low intelligence will tend to emphasize mating effort. Criminal behavior essentially represents the most direct and immediate ways of getting valued resources, and to be successful at it requires a willingness to risk retaliation from victims.

Evolutionary Expropriative Theory

Lawrence Cohen, Richard Machalek, and Bryan Vila (Cohen & Machalek, 1988; Vila & Cohen, 1993; Vila, 1994, 1997) have proposed an evolutionary theory that shares with conditional adaptation theory the assumption that from a genetic standpoint, all humans have an equal potential for antisocial behavior. According to the evolutionary expropriative theory, genes incline all of us to organize our lives around acquiring resources that will help us to reproduce. Two extreme approaches to obtaining resources are identified: productive (or generative) and expropriative. A productive means of acquiring resources involves creating resources from more fundamental elements, often in cooperation with others. The expropriative strategy involves manipulating and victimizing others to acquire resources, often taking advantage of the work of others, such as through stealing and tricking them. Antisocial or criminal behavior represents the main forms of expropriative strategies.

The theory asserts that people engage in crime as a reaction to not having access to adequate resources (i.e., resource deprivation) or in anticipation of a lack of resources in the future. Unlike the conditional adaptation theory, there is no critical time during childhood when these calculations are made. Instead, people make their assessments throughout life depending upon the environmental conditions presented them. Theoretically, as the number of humans comprising a society grows, so too do opportunities for expropriative tactics. Accordingly, the theory contends that victims of expropriative tactics in a rapidly growing, organized society often attempt to retaliate, either individually or collectively, giving rise to the criminal justice system.

Overall, evolutionary theories of criminal and antisocial behavior attempt to explain such behavior in terms of its long-term reproductive consequences. Two of the theories—the r/K theory and alternative adaptation theory— assume that genes act differently on people's tendencies to engage in antisocial behavior. Two other theories—conditional adaptation theory and evolutionary expropriative theory—assume that genes incline everyone to adjust their behavior to environmental circumstances in ways that make some people more likely than others to exhibit antisocial tendencies. The other theory—the cheater theory—assumes that two types of criminals/psychopaths have evolved: ones that are genetically hard-wired and ones that largely learn their offending behavior. The latter are thought to be more likely to abandon their criminal behavior by the time they reach adulthood than are the former.

Evolutionary theories have been controversial for several reasons. They appear to consider human behavior in the same context as animals that are less complex with respect to their origins, motivations, and behaviors. These theories do not appear to account for differences between human individuals in their intentions and behaviors that arise irrespective of widescale environmental conditions. Evolutionary variables are also not concrete and researchers are not able to directly manipulate them to test their theories. Nevertheless, there are obvious parallels between evolutionary theories and what is often observed among humans in their natural environments, which vary tremendously with respect to criminogenic characteristics. Because our genetic structure and function act as a go-between for evolutionary factors to theoretically influence behavior, a short but detailed discussion follows to summarize an ever-growing body of research on genetic contributions to various dimensions of antisocial behavior.

GENETICS

Evolution has dictated that the brain has a particular purpose which is to protect the individual and its offspring in its environment and to ensure that its genes are reproduced. In addition to the brain's vital functions that control movement and senses, it regulates behavior. Through the brain's influence over behavior, the individual can be more assured of survival through reproduction and other ways of adapting to a constantly changing environment. Thus, the more complex the brain is, the more ability an individual will have to develop various adaptive responses. In order to understand how the brain regulates behavior and what mechanisms go awry when behavior becomes poorly regulated, a familiarity with genetic factors that design the brain to influence behavior is necessary. Individuals who exhibit patterns of adaptive behaviors may be thought to possess optimal, complex and efficient brain function. Brain function may be compromised, on the other hand, in individuals who exhibit poor self-control over their behavior.

Individuals are vulnerable in different ways and through different underlying mechanisms to antisocial behavior; interactions between genetic and environmental sources of variation underlie these individual differences. Identification of genetic contributions does not reduce behavior to a gene level, but can help explain the origins of variation in behavior within a population. Because the focus of the majority of research on deviant behavior has been on social and environmental sources, the domain of this chapter is research on genetic factors that may increase or decrease risk. Specifically, the role of genetics in affecting behaviors that centrally involve impulse control and negative mood state is summarized since these two traits are so highly correlated with criminal activity. According to this view, genetic factors help to explain individual vulnerability to certain behavioral patterns or orientations. Nevertheless, other factors such as choice and voluntary actions are more important in explaining behavior on a population-wide scale.

In terms of public policy, treatment, prevention, and research aimed at identifying specific genes in antisocial behavior, the level of genetic influence is less important than the ability of this science to enhance understanding of the underlying processes and particular vulnerabilities and needs of individuals. In other words, knowing that impulsivity is, say, 60 percent genetic in the population tells us nothing about any given individual's predisposition. It is much more useful to know which environmental, biological, and genetic factors are contributing to behavioral problems in a single individual so that appropriate and effective treatment or prevention measures can be taken.

Heritability Studies

Heritability studies estimate the minimum extent to which variation between individuals in a trait within a particular human population is genetically determined. For example, IQ is considered to be highly heritable based on the extent to which identical (monozygotic) twins are more similar in IQ than fraternal (dizygotic) twins. Because identical twins are 100 percent genetically similar and fraternal twins only 50 percent similar, a higher rate of *concordance,* or similarity, in a behavioral trait between identical twins than fraternal twins indicates that the genetic influence is significant. Thus, the levels and ratios of concordance rates in identical and fraternal twins are used to estimate heritability (see Figure 3–1).

In adoption studies, concordance rates are compared for children and their biological parents relative to children and their adoptive parents. Given that children and their biological parents are 50 percent genetically identical by descent, while adopted children are unrelated to their adoptive parents, higher concordance rates between biological parents and their adopted-away children indicates a genetic influence on the trait. On the other hand, when concordance rates are higher between adoptive parents and their adoptees than they are between biological parents and their children, that indicates that environment, modeling, and learning may have more to do with the trait than genetics (see Figure 3–2).

Heritability studies of various dimensions of criminal behavior have most often focused on impulsivity, aggressiveness, and antisocial personality disorder. Such *phenotypic* traits are more likely to be genetically influenced than the more complex, socially bound concepts of criminality and violence. However, high heritability for a trait in a population does not mean that environmental influences cannot be identified nor that psychosocial prevention or treatment strategies cannot be effective. There may be inclination toward a particular behavioral pattern, but not predestination, so that even traits with genetic roots are not unchangeable and can be manipulated using environmental approaches. Nevertheless, inborn differences are a starting point for understanding the web of interactions that leads to complex traits, including impulsive-aggression and other antisocial behaviors.

Identical Twins

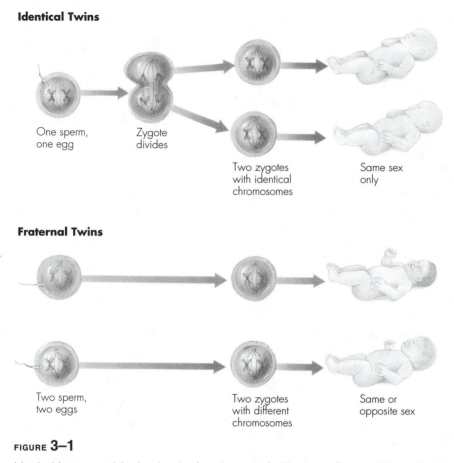

One sperm,   Zygote
one egg   divides

                                        Two zygotes   Same sex
                                        with identical   only
                                        chromosomes

Fraternal Twins

Two sperm,   Two zygotes   Same or
two eggs   with different   opposite sex
                                       chromosomes

FIGURE **3—1**

Identical (monozygotic) twins develop from the same fertilized egg. Fraternal (dizygotic) twins grow from two eggs fertilized by two different sperm.

From *Introduction to Psychology,* 5th edition, by J. W. Kalat. Copyright © 1999 by Brooks/Cole. Used by permission.

According to heritability studies, the extent of genetic influence is surprisingly high for behavioral traits, particularly alcoholism, impulsivity, and various other dimensions of antisocial behavior. One might think that traits such as these would not be measurably influenced by genetic factors because they are, in reality, crudely estimated and strongly influenced by cross-cultural and other environmental factors. However, data from large, methodologically sound twin and adoption studies, too numerous to review here, suggest that traits related to repetitive aggressive behavior (e.g., impulsivity, negative affect, drug abuse, alcoholism, and cognitive deficits) are significantly heritable (e.g., see Brennan et al., 1996; Gottesman & Goldsmith, 1994; Carey, 1995; Coccaro et al., 1993; Rowe, 1983). Furthermore, similar findings have been reported for the heritability of personality factors, like extroversion, in-

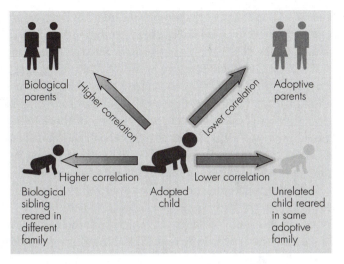

FIGURE **3—2**

The IQ scores of adopted children correlate more highly with those of their biological relatives than with those of their adoptive relatives. Such data point to a probable role of heredity.

From *Introduction to Psychology,* 5th edition, by J. W. Kalat. Copyright © 1999 by Brooks/Cole. Used by permission.

troversion, cognitive deficits, conduct disorder, or anxiety, which are strongly predictive of both substance abuse and aggression (see Fishbein, 1999).

Molecular Genetic Studies: Assessing and Evaluating Genetic Effects

While findings suggest that traits associated with impulsivity, aggressiveness, and alcoholism have significant heritability, twin and adoption studies do not identify the genetically influenced biological mechanisms that may contribute to these traits. New techniques in molecular genetics have resulted in important discoveries that suggest that certain biological systems are involved in these disorders. These efforts are now being devoted to identifying the specific genes that may be influential in producing relevant traits, like impulsivity. Although there have been some false starts in identifying specific genes for behavioral disorders, the field is very active.

Characteristics of genes that have been linked to psychological and behavioral traits are called *markers;* they "mark" a location of genes that may be actively involved in contributing to a trait. Genetic *variants* are structural differences in genes, also called *polymorphisms.* Eventually, when variants and markers have been identified for relevant traits, we will understand better how genes are expressed, or become active, in response to environmental input, and how their activity (or lack thereof) contributes to a behavioral trait.

Thus, in the same way that a genetic polymorphism gives rise to different blood types (O, A, B, AB), specific genes have been tentatively linked to particular behavioral traits, some of which are associated with increased risk to crime (Comings et al., 1996; Goldman et al., 1996; Rowe et al., 1998a). It is clear that any given gene associated with high risk traits is not "abnormal" per se; it may be present in many individuals throughout the population. What is important to remember is that individuals who carry a number of these genes appear to be at higher risk for antisocial behavior and other behavioral difficulties—they may be considered "genetically loaded." Once again, though, environment contributes to the expression of these genes and plays a critical role as to whether the resulting behavior is actually antisocial or another more socially accepted, albeit at times impulsive or bad tempered, behavioral pattern.

The genetic markers and variants most often related to behavioral disorders involve the way neurotransmitters, like dopamine and serotonin, are made, metabolized, and interact with their brain *receptors*. Receptors are sites in the brain that receive particular chemicals and enable them to become active (Comings, 1995; Volavka, 1995). Too few or too many receptors, or a deviation in the way they function, can alter neurotransmitter activity levels in the brain. Thus, levels of neurotransmitter activity and metabolism are to a great extent genetically determined (see Figure 3–3).

In addition to neurotransmitters, certain enzymes also play an important role in behavioral traits. Enzymes break down or degrade chemicals in the brain as part of their metabolism. For example, the breakdown of dopamine and serotonin into their metabolic end-products is coordinated by two forms of the enzyme *monoamine oxidase*, MAOA and MAOB. As you will learn later, deviations in the activity of these enzymes have been associated with certain behavioral and temperamental difficulties.

In addition to neurotransmitter function, differences in the structure and activity of hormone receptors in antisocial behavior are also being investigated through genetic analysis. Levels of these enzymes and hormones have also been associated with the behavioral phenotypes impulsivity and aggressiveness, as discussed in the following chapter.

A variety of genetically influenced psychiatric disorders are accompanied by increased liabilities for impulsive and aggressive behaviors, including Antisocial Personality Disorder, Conduct Disorder, Attention Deficit Disorder, and Borderline Personality Disorder (Coccaro et al., 1993; Rowe et al., 1998b). Alcoholism, believed to be largely genetic (Goldman, 1993), is also related to susceptibility to impulsive and aggressive behaviors. Aggressive behavior is frequently triggered by intake of relatively small amounts of alcohol, and more than half of violent crimes occur under the influence of alcohol (see Reiss & Roth, 1993). The early-onset subtype of alcoholism, Type II alcoholism (shown in Table 3–1), is itself considered to be genetically influenced

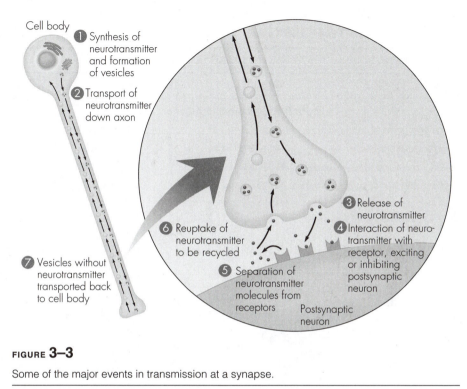

Cell body

① Synthesis of neurotransmitter and formation of vesicles

② Transport of neurotransmitter down axon

③ Release of neurotransmitter

④ Interaction of neurotransmitter with receptor, exciting or inhibiting postsynaptic neuron

⑤ Separation of neurotransmitter molecules from receptors

⑥ Reuptake of neurotransmitter to be recycled

⑦ Vesicles without neurotransmitter transported back to cell body

Postsynaptic neuron

FIGURE **3–3**

Some of the major events in transmission at a synapse.

From *Biological Psychology*, by J.W. Kalat. Copyright © 1998 by Brooks/Cole. Used by permission.

and is associated with antisocial behavior and impulsiveness (Cloninger et al., 1981; von Knorring et al., 1987). There are many other associations that have been made between aggressive behavior and genetically influenced psychiatric diagnoses. Psychiatric disorders that are, in part, characterized by an increased risk for aggression include suicide in depression (Tsuang, 1983), schizophrenia (Gottesman & Shields, 1982), alcoholism (Niskanen & Achte, 1972; Tsuang, 1983), self-directed violence in borderline personality disorder, and self-destructive behaviors in Lesch-Nyhan syndrome (a male disease characterized by mental retardation, cerebral palsy, and self-mutilating behaviors). Therefore, identification of genetic factors that influence these disorders would contribute to an understanding of the mechanisms involved in aggressive behavior.

We are just beginning to identify some of the variants and markers for neurotransmitter (e.g., dopamine and serotonin), enzyme (e.g., MAOA), and hormone (e.g., thyroid hormone receptors; Hauser et al., 1993) function that may be associated with impulsive aggression and related disorders. Researchers are encouraged by the possibility that scanning for additional

| TABLE 3–1 | TRAITS OF TYPE I AND TYPE II ALCOHOLICS |

Characteristics	Alcoholic Type	
	Type I	**Type II**
Problems Related to Alcohol		
Common age of onset	After 25	Before 25
Gender most afflicted	Male and female	Mostly male
Severity of alcohol dependence	Relatively mild	Unable to abstain
Fighting and arrests when drinking	Not common	Very common to be violent with or without alcohol
Psychological dependence (loss of control over drinking)	High	Not common
Guilt and fear about drinking problem	Common	Not common
Inheritance	Questionable	Most likely through father
Other drug use	Less common	More common
Personality Traits		
Reward dependence	High	Low
Eager to please		
Sensitive		
Dependent		
Harm avoidance	High	Low
Cautious		
Inhibited and shy		
Novelty seeking	Low	High
Impulsive		
Excitable		
Distractible		
Family History		
Criminal history	Less common	Common (especially father)
Treatment		
Effectiveness	More successful	Resistant to treatment

Two types of alcoholism have been proposed by Cloninger. Type I occurs later in life, is less insidious, is not as often associated with criminality, and is not believed to be strongly genetically influenced. Type II alcoholism, on the other hand, occurs earlier in life, is more destructive, is more often associated with criminality, and is believed to be largely inherited.

candidate genes will detect sets of genetic variants at a given gene, called *alleles*, significant for antisocial behaviors. It is important to recognize that these genes will be scanned and the variants detected independent of any research program specifically directed toward criminality or antisocial personality disorder. Direct gene analyses have revealed genetic variants, many of them common, at most of the dopamine and serotonin-related genes previously implicated in impulsive and aggressive behavior.

SUMMARY

The research presented in this chapter supports the following conclusions: (1) All human behavior has a genetic component. (2) There are no genes or biological causes of specific human behaviors. Instead, genes help to design our temperament and personality, and provide an orientation or predisposition to behave according to certain patterns. (3) Expression of genetic and biological traits can be modified by the environment. No one is predestined to behave in a certain way or to commit crime. (4) On a global level, social and economic deprivation, deleterious environmental conditions, psychological trauma, and abuse lead to antisocial behavior. Deterioration of inner cities and dissolution of resources that would otherwise have protective effects are substantially contributory. Because social influences are known, effective interventions can be implemented now. (5) Vulnerabilities to antisocial behavior cross all boundaries, but will be most abundant where the social risks are highest.

The chapter that follows discusses the neurochemical, physiological, and neuropsychological mechanisms through which genes involved in behavioral vulnerabilities are believed to be expressed. Before entering this discussion, two critical points that condition the relationship between genetic traits and behavioral outcomes should be noted. First, for any given individual, there is a range of potential responses to environmental inputs that are genetically determined and regulated by chemical and physiological systems in the brain. Within this range, many environmental influences play a role in determining which portion of the spectrum of responses will be expressed. With this in mind, we see that many behavioral outcomes are possible at any given time; each situation is unique, although consistent experiences (e.g., adverse or positive) will be cumulative to produce predictable and consistent patterns of behavior. Second, biological functions are substantially influenced by environmental factors and cannot always be directly attributed to genetic traits (i.e., genotype). The social and physical environment have the potential to significantly alter brain function irrespective of genetic features; example, traumatic experiences disrupt neurotransmitter function, hormonal release, and neuropsychological development. Importantly, as will be discussed in Chapter 5, our temperament, which has significant roots in our genes, can also alter environmental responses to the individual, thereby either exacerbating or suppressing the behavioral outcome (e.g., irritability or negative emotionality in an infant can elicit more severe parenting responses, thereby compounding the child's difficulties; see Moffitt, 1993).

BIOBEHAVIORAL RESEARCH

4

Brain Chemistry and Function

Brain function is a result of interactive influences from our genes and our environment. While genes set the stage for individual potential and range of possible responses and behaviors, the environment helps to determine how that will actually be expressed and ways in which behavior will fluctuate over time. It is the function of our brains that gives rise to our emotions, moods, drives, memories, intelligence, personality, and much more. Accordingly, there is no way to study the complexities of human behavior without including the central role of the brain. In this chapter, various aspects of brain function are discussed: biochemistry, psychophysiology, neuropsychology, as well as anatomy and other functions that are highlighted by imaging studies. Each of these subsections describes brain functions, related to propensity for antisocial behavior, that reflect the expression of genes as they are influenced by the environment. In the concluding section, a discussion of developmental processes that contribute to fluctuations in behavioral patterns throughout the life span is presented. This section emphasizes that not only is behavior changeable via sheer willpower, but that aspects of brain function that influence our behavior can be altered through both biological and environmental manipulations.

BIOCHEMISTRY

There are many aspects of biochemistry that influence human behavior, and each one operates through effects on the central (the brain and spinal cord; CNS) and peripheral (e.g., the "autonomic" portion; ANS) nervous systems. Neurotransmitters are chemical messengers that convey "information" in the form of an electrically charged signal from neuron to neuron, and from brain structure to brain structure. The balance of neurotransmitters, and their metabolism and activity levels are partially a function of genetics, but are also directly affected by environmental and psychosocial conditions. In general,

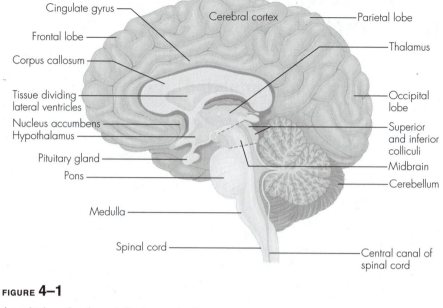

FIGURE 4–1

A sagittal section through the human brain.

Source: After Nieuwenhuys, Voogd, & vanHuijzen, 1988.

neurotransmitters regulate emotion, mood, hunger, thirst, sleep, and a host of other behavioral and psychological processes. Certain enzymes influence neurotransmitter activity primarily by degrading or breaking down neurotransmitters in a natural metabolic process. Hormones, in contrast, are chemicals released by glands that travel to various parts of the brain and body to exert their effects. For purposes of this discussion, hormones of interest can be categorized as either "sex" or "stress" hormones; they regulate sex drive, reproductive functions, aggression, territoriality, sexual differentiation, responses to environmental stimuli, and energy levels. The location in the brain where all these substances are most concentrated determines, to great extent, what brain functions are affected when these chemicals are active (see Figure 4–1).

Neurotransmitters

Current studies of biochemical mechanisms underlying various dimensions of antisocial behavior focus on the role of central neurotransmitter systems in regulating impulse control and activity levels—or arousal of the nervous system. The neurotransmitters dopamine and serotonin have been strongly and consistently associated with aggressive behaviors, even in the absence of a disorder, per se. Thus, a particular concentration of this section is on these neurotransmitters.

Dopamine The dopamine system affects an individual's ability to respond to "cues" in the environment. Cues are either events or objects that have been experienced along with some sort of reward or stimulus that satisfies some drive. When a cue is paired with a reward or satisfying object, that cue becomes associated with the reward, and produces a "conditioned response"; thus, the individual is likely to repeat the behavior that's associated with the reward, with the expectation that he/she will obtain the reward or satisfying stimulus as a result. For example, when something potentially useful is nearby, like food or a potential mate, dopamine activity sets into motion a biological process that gives rise to an emotional response that motivates behavior. As a result, the individual is motivated by dopamine's actions to explore the options that will allow the individual to obtain the reward. Excitement, anxiety, curiosity, or pleasure are the emotions that provide fuel for "flight or fight" responses, exploration of something novel, or avoidance of something unpleasant. Thus, when the dopamine system is activated, novelty seeking and self-stimulation behaviors increase. When this system goes awry, however, behavior may be activated in the absence of a reward, a threat, or other appropriate stimulus. This "approach system" can "produce . . . dangerous asocial and disruptive behavior" (Pihl & Petersen, 1995: 385) when it is activated in the absence of an appropriate social setting or provocation.

The dopamine system has been implicated in displays of aggressive or violent behavior. Dopamine metabolism increases when laboratory animals are provoked to behave aggressively (Cases et al., 1995). In humans, the overproduction of dopamine has been associated with psychotic behavior, and has been linked to antisocial behavior and violence (Gabel et al., 1995; Tiihonen et al., 1995). Antipsychotic drugs that decrease dopamine levels tend to decrease fighting behaviors (see Raine, 1993: 85). Nevertheless, meta-analyses (analysis of the results of many studies combined) of neurotransmitter levels in various samples of people with antisocial behavior show inconsistencies between studies and no direct effects of dopamine on aggression (Raine, 1993). The lack of consistent findings may be due to differences in populations studied and in the ways antisocial behavior was defined. Moreover, main effects of dopamine have been examined rather than evaluating the interaction of dopamine with other neurotransmitter systems that influence behavior, so we do not have a complete picture of how neurotransmitters work together.

Serotonin An abnormally low level of serotonergic activity[2] is regarded as another significant player in influencing impulsive-aggressive behavior (Muhlbauer, 1985; Soubrie, 1986; van Praag et al., 1987). Stimulation to brain

---

[2]Low levels of serotonergic function can result from various causes, from genetic defects to environmental stressors.

regions concentrated with serotonin produce feelings of pleasure, for example, the septum. Also, lesions that switch off areas of the brain that are dense with serotonin connections produce rage and attack behaviors. Genetic strains of mice that show lower serotonin activity than other strains are more aggressive and aggression is suppressed when serotonin metabolism is blocked, resulting in increased serotonergic activation (Cases et al., 1995).

Initial research on serotonin in humans was intriguing and led investigators on a search to identify its precise role in various psychiatric disorders. In one of the first studies, postmortem examinations of the brain showed low levels of serotonin in people who had committed suicide, suggesting that serotonin deficiency was related to depression. However, these findings were not uniform. Specifically, those who committed a violent suicide (e.g., using a gun or knife) had lower levels of serotonin in the brain than those who committed a "nonviolent" suicide (e.g., using pills or gas) (Brown et al., 1982). This important study led researchers to believe that low serotonin activity was not only associated with depression and suicide, but suggested that it may also be involved in violent behavior. Scores of additional studies found support for this possibility by reporting several indicators of lowered serotonin activity in studies of juveniles and adults characterized as violent or impulsive, in contrast to those who are not (Coccaro et al., 1993; Coccaro & Murphy, 1991; Fishbein et al., 1989a; Kruesi et al., 1992; Linnoila et al., 1983; Moss, et al., 1990; Schalling, 1993; Virkkunen & Linnoila, 1993; Virkkunen et al., 1994a, 1994b). With further refinements to these investigations, however, it became clear that serotonin was more specifically responsible for regulating impulse control than simply aggressive behavior. Implications of these findings are that when serotonin activity levels are relatively low, the tendency or predisposition to behave in certain ways (e.g., aggression), that may be related to the existence of certain personality traits (e.g., negative or hostile mood), is more likely to be exhibited. For example, in the presence of depression, suicide becomes more likely, while in the presence of anger and hostility, violence becomes more likely. Put simply, a deficit in serotonin activity jeopardizes the ability to inhibit urges, increasing the likelihood that underlying hostility or negative mood will lead to aggression or another inappropriate behavior.

There is another related body of research suggesting that serotonin may influence excessive alcohol drinking and possibly also alcoholism. These findings are particularly interesting in light of reports that impulsive and violent individuals have also shown low serotonin activity levels and are prone to antisocial behavior while drinking (Coccaro & Murphy, 1991; Linnoila et al., 1994; Roy et al., 1987; Virkkunen, 1983; Virkkunen & Linnoila, 1990). A drop in serotonin activity may be partially responsible for the lack of ability to inhibit behavior and impulsive urges when drinking alcohol, leading to violent behavior in susceptible people (Buydens-Branchey et al., 1989). There is a subgroup of alcoholics that is believed to be at genetic risk for aggressiveness or other forms of criminality (Cloninger, 1987), and some speculation that both their alcoholism and antisocial behavior may be influenced by a preexisting deficit in serotonin function. When drinking, such individuals are more likely to feel hostile and negative, and display impulsive-aggressive behavior because, theoretically, alcohol lowers serotonin activity even more in individuals who already have deficiencies in serotonin. As serotonin activity drops during alcohol consumption, dopamine activity rises, leading to both a loss in impulse control and the expression of any violent tendencies the drinker may have. The use of treatments that stimulate serotonin activity in such cases may be helpful for co-occurring alcoholism and violence by reducing (1) depression and/or anxiety, (2) alcohol craving, (3) some of the reinforcing properties of alcohol, and (4) aggressiveness (see Brizer, 1988).

Norepinephrine (Noradrenaline)   Norepinephrine (NE) is a neurotransmitter that is produced from dopamine; dopamine is converted to NE through the action of the enzyme, dopamine beta-hydroxylase. If there is too much NE in the brain, it is destroyed by the enzyme monoamine oxidase (see the following discussion) and MHPG (3,4 dihydroxyphenylglycol) is the left over by-product. NE has been of particular interest due to its involvement in stress responses, emotions, attention, and arousal. It plays a primary role in the so-called "fight and flight" response by causing the release of stress hormones from the adrenal glands, and exciting the central and peripheral nervous systems. NE activates the fight and flight response by stimulating various brain structures, from the frontal cortex, to the limbic system (a primitive part of the brain controlling emotions and survival functions), to the brain stem (Wallace et al., 1992). (See Figure 4–2.)

Significant changes in NE have been documented during preparation for, execution of, and recovery from activities that involve states of high arousal, including violent behavior (Miczek et al., 1994). While NE activity is related to states of arousal, mood, and behavioral activation, NE activity is not predictive of particular behavioral outcomes; rather, it may relate to patterns of behavior or a particular orientation to the environment, such as tendencies toward impulsivity, sensation-seeking, or high activity levels. For example, NE activation as a result of amphetamine use is strongly associated with agitation and aggression, but the actual behavioral outcome depends upon the circumstance, setting, and individual predisposition.

Several studies have established a link between violence and NE and its by-product MHPG (Brown et al., 1979; Magnusson, 1987, 1988; Woodman, 1979; Woodman & Hinton, 1978), although there are studies that did not find support for this link (Bioulac et al., 1980; Linnoila et al., 1983). Drugs that increase NE activity are known to worsen violence in patients who are already agitated (Rampling, 1978). Directionality has been an unresolved issue when relating NE levels to violence. The majority of studies indicate that higher

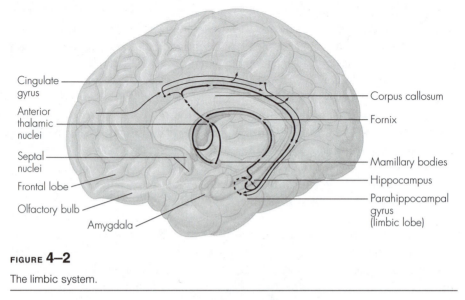

FIGURE **4–2**

The limbic system.

Source: Based on Maclean, 1949.

levels of NE are associated with aggression and violence; however, because NE values are highly variable, the most promising approach for the use of NE levels as a marker for violence is under conditions of stress or provocation, rather than a resting state. For example, instead of sitting in an armchair in a laboratory while blood is taken, the individual would be provoked or stimulated in some way while blood is extracted so that changes in NE can be monitored—this technique produces more similar responses to those in the real world. Nevertheless, it is unknown at the present time what the precise role of NE is in contributing to violence. But because NE activity levels are suppressed by medications that are used in the treatment of violence (Eichelman, 1986; Elliott, 1977; Ratey et al., 1986, 1987), there are clear indications that NE's role in violence is significant. Also, it is important to note that NE's effects are highly dependent on its interaction with other central neurotransmitters and environmental conditions.

Monoamine Oxidase   Monoamine oxidase (MAO), an enzyme responsible for the breakdown of several neurotransmitters (e.g., dopamine, serotonin, and norepinephrine), is involved in several aspects of brain function by its regulation of neurotransmitter concentrations and activity levels. MAO helps to flush used neurotransmitter molecules from the nervous system. While the range of optimal MAO levels is rather large, unusually high or low levels are believed to adversely affect social behaviors. Low MAO activity results in excessive levels of dopamine and norepinephrine which are believed to contribute to aggression, loss of self control, and inappropriate motivations to behave (discussed earlier). Because MAO concentrations within the brain are particularly high in areas involved in complex thinking processes, affect and mood state, impulse control, and aggressiveness (the brain stem, hypothalamus, and prefrontal cortex), the relationship between irregularities in its activity and possible effects on social and emotional behaviors is understandable.

For two decades, irregularities in MAO levels have been linked with antisocial behaviors, particularly those involving psychopathy, aggression, and violent behavior (see Ellis, 1992). Several studies have related variations in MAO activity to tendencies toward alcoholism, sensation-seeking behavior, and impulsivity (see Hsu et al., 1989); psychopathy (Lidberg et al., 1985); and excessive alcohol use, often associated with antisocial behavior (Dolinski et al., 1985; Faraj et al., 1987; Oreland et al., 1983). Low MAO levels were found in male student volunteers with histories of psychosocial problems, including convictions for various offenses (Schalling et al., 1987) and among relatives of low-MAO subjects (Buchsbaum et al., 1976).

One recent study of a large Dutch family spanning four generations found fourteen males to be affected by a complex behavioral syndrome that includes borderline mental retardation and severely impulsive aggressive behavior (Brunner et al., 1993a, 1993b). Examples of their behavior include arson, rape, threats of murder, and actual attempts to take a person's life. A genetic defect was discovered in affected males and found to be associated with abnormalities in MAO metabolism. In this disorder, MAO levels are too low to effectively metabolize dopamine and norepinephrine so these neurotransmitters accumulate in the brain and contribute to excessive behaviors. Because this defect is rare, it is impossible to relate these findings to other families in which impulsive aggression appears prevalent. Nevertheless, investigators are considering the possibility that subtler forms of MAO deficiency may exist in a subgroup of the population that exhibits these behaviors, although the causal relationship between a MAO metabolic abnormality and behavioral disturbance is not a simple one (Brunner, 1996).

Hormones

A large body of literature reflecting both animal and human studies conducted over the past decade reports an association between aggressiveness and various "sex" and "stress" hormones. Animal studies are briefly mentioned because they provide the models for human investigation. However, the focus of this section is on human studies since the literature contains some inconsistencies between human and animal findings, indicating that making blanket comparisons between species is unjustifiable. The most informative studies of the role of hormones in human behavior include either a pharmacological challenge (e.g., the administration of a drug that either suppresses or enhances the release of a particular hormone or set of hormones) or a behavioral challenge (e.g., provoking anger under laboratory conditions or inducing a stressful state) to identify group differences in hormonal responses. Nevertheless, reports also suggest that levels of hormones when the individual is in a resting state also often differ between subjects with and without various behavioral and psychological disorders (Guerri et al., 1998).

Sex Hormones   The most studied hormones in relation to aggression are testosterone and other male hormones, called androgens. Females produce testosterone in lower amounts and with somewhat differing effects. Animal studies suggest that testosterone increases aggression (Archer, 1991), although findings of an association from human studies have not been as consistent. Studies of people with a disorder (congenital adrenal hyperplasia) caused by exposure to high levels of androgens in prenatal and early postnatal periods, provide evidence for testosterone's role in aggression—these people tend to be unusually aggressive (Berenbaum & Resnick, 1997). Testosterone concentrations correlated positively with self-rated measures of aggression in nonpsychiatric subjects and were reported to be higher in alcoholics with a chronic history of domestic violence (Bergman & Brismar, 1994). Studies have consistently found evidence for elevated saliva testosterone levels[3] in both male and female violent offenders relative to controls (Banks & Dabbs, 1996; Dabbs & Hargrove, 1997) and in cerebrospinal fluid (van Goozen et al., 1998; Virkkunen et al., 1996), suggesting a role for testosterone in criminal violence and aggressive dominance. In a laboratory investigation of normal male subjects, the administration of testosterone resulted in a significantly higher level of aggressive behavior relative to placebo (Kouri et al., 1995). Interestingly, Higley et al. (1996) found that high levels of testosterone raised rates and intensity of aggression in people with low serotonin activity; their interactive effects on aggression were significant. (See Figure 4–3.)

Overall, data from both animals and humans suggest that the biological and behavioral reactions to male hormones often involve aggression. We do not know, however, which is the chicken and which is the egg in all circumstances and in all people. Behaviors that have been associated with elevated testosterone levels are substantially context-dependent (Rubinow & Schmidt, 1996); in other words, high levels of testosterone are not always associated with aggression—outcomes depend on the social circumstances and the person's characteristics. Also, these hormones not only influence dominance and aggressive behavior, but they also are known to increase their activity *in response* to behaving that way (Mazur & Booth, 1998). Once again, in other words, behaving in an aggressive way can *lead to* increases in testosterone.

---

[3]Hormone levels can be inexpensively assessed in the saliva.

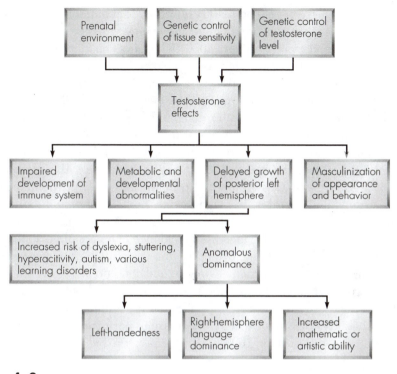

FIGURE 4–3

Summary of hypothesis on testosterone effects.

Source: Based on Geschwind & Galaburda 1985; McManus & Bryden, 1991.

Thus, it is necessary for research to show us what circumstances and types of individuals are most affected by sex hormones, and to help us to better understand the nature of the causal chain.

Biological or integrated studies of aggressive or antisocial females are scarce, such that general conclusions about underlying mechanisms cannot be made. There is some evidence, however, for the role of irregularities in sex hormone levels in female antisocial behavior. Female fetuses that are exposed to high levels of androgens, or a hypersensitivity in the brain to these hormones, during prenatal development can *masculinize* the fetus by altering the developing neuroanatomy and physical constitution (Ellis & Ames, 1987; Nyborg, 1984; Simon & Whalen, 1986). Traits such as excessive facial hair, unusually large muscle mass, deep voice, underdeveloped breasts, and a larger lower body can be due to the influence of male hormones on the female constitution. Strong evidence exists for the influence of male hormones on a masculine physique, a masculine self-identity, and increased aggressiveness in adult females (see Ellis, 1987b, 1988; and Fishbein, 1992). A tour of a female correctional facility bears witness to the relationship between male hormones and aggression where it may be readily observed that a much larger number of females are constitutionally masculine and hyperaggressive relative to those in the general population (Fishbein, 2000). This effect cannot be due to social experiences, but must be a result of some biological process.

Prenatal drug exposures, genetic defects, neurotransmitter imbalances, certain medical conditions and even social factors can all affect sexual and social development by altering sex hormone influences. Dabbs and colleagues, for example, have reported high levels of testosterone among violent female inmates and delinquents relative to those considered nonviolent (Banks & Dabbs, 1996; Dabbs & Hargrove, 1997; Dabbs et al., 1988). Also, females exposed to high levels of androgen in the prenatal and early postnatal periods (due to a congenital disorder) had significantly higher aggression scores than controls (Berenbaum & Resnick, 1997). Unusually high testosterone levels in females may contribute to the increased incidence of a masculine appearance (Fishbein, 2000) among female offenders and may function to reinforce aggressive tendencies under certain environmental conditions. Interestingly, giving androgens to female who are not involved in criminal behavior has been clearly associated with an increase in aggression proneness, sexual arousability and spatial ability performance, and a decrease in performance on verbal fluency tasks (van Goozen et al., 1995).

Stress Hormones   Certain hormones are released in response to signals from the hypothalamus, in a primitive area of the brain, and secreted by the pituitary and adrenal glands. These hormones are known to be exquisitely sensitive to both psychosocial stressors and novel situations; thus, they are referred to as stress hormones (e.g., ACTH (adrenocorticotropic hormone), cortisol, prolactin). In general, studies report increased cortisol activity in individuals with unusually heightened reactions to challenging situations, and an increased incidence in conduct disordered behavior and depression (see Susman & Ponirakis, 1997 for review). These findings suggest that some people, as a result of predisposition or social experiences, are more sensitive to stress and have a greater biological reaction to it.

On the other hand, low cortisol responses to stressful stimuli may reflect low levels of nervous system arousal. Low cortisol levels have been found to characterize people considered to be psychopathic, aggressive, and who have post-traumatic stress disorder (Raine et al., 1997a). Consistent with that possibility is research showing low concentrations of cortisol in aggressive youth (Susman et al., 1991; Tennes & Kreye, 1985) and violent adult offenders (Virkkunen, 1985) who lack anxiety (see Raine, 1993 for review). If biological responses to stressful stimuli do not occur as they should, then the individual may be relatively insensitive to stress and may either not cope well with it, or may not be conditioned adequately to avoid it (see the following discussion of psychopathy).

Alcohol consumption may further strengthen the link between stress hormones and antisocial behavior, but possibly in the opposite direction. For example, Buydens and Branchey (1992) found increased levels of cortisol in violent alcoholics relative to control subjects, suggesting a relationship between impulsive violence and heightened stress responses.

PSYCHOPHYSIOLOGICAL CORRELATES

Differences in physiological activity of the nervous system have been found between people with and without violence and drug abuse (see Fishbein, 1990, 1991; Raine, 1993). These differences may arise from genetic factors, or people may develop physiological irregularities as a result of environmental experiences. Either way, they often reflect an underlying dysfunction of neurotransmitter systems. Although inconsistencies in findings exist due to differences in methodologies, measures, and subjects, numerous studies suggest that stimulation-seeking, impulsivity, aggressiveness, hyperactivity, attention deficit hyperactivity disorder (ADHD), lack of avoidance responses, and inability to empathize are behavioral correlates of serotonin and dopamine system abnormalities with measurable psychophysiological consequences. Most of the evidence supports the notion that individuals prone to violence, psychopathy, and/or drug abuse have unusually low physiological levels of CNS and ANS activity, which appear to be related to high levels of sensation-seeking (see Pallone & Hennessy, 1996). How is the physiological activity of the nervous system related to sensation-seeking and high-risk behaviors? The following section attempts to answer that question by describing the function of the ANS and presenting research findings that may eventually help us to better understand this relationship.

Behavior, Stress, and the Autonomic Nervous System

Imagine that you are walking through a dark alley and you realize that someone is quickly approaching. Various physiological and biochemical responses occur that involve activation of the "flight or fight" mechanism. The first step in the flight and fight mechanism is the perception by the cortex (the gray matter in charge of higher intellectual functions) of the event. This is called *cognition,* part of the thinking process. The cortex "talks" to various structures, including memory centers of the limbic system, using chemical and electrical signals that help the individual to quickly *remember* the dangerous nature of such a situation. Subsequently, the brain will begin to *reason* or determine the best plan of action. And the motor system becomes active to initiate the necessary motions for *coping.* As a result of this biochemical and physiological process, the limbic system becomes highly activated to instill feelings of *fear* or urgency. Such feelings are necessary to mobilize action within the body for successful survival. Without fear or a sense of urgency, we are likely to be sluggish in our response, which is not good from a survival perspective! The limbic system then activates the ANS to produce several physiological responses all designed to mobilize the energy and motivation to cope quickly, including:

- Skin electricity heightens
- Digestion slows
- Heart rate speeds up
- Blood pressure rises
- Glucose in the brain increases
- Oxygen to the muscles and brain increases
- Bronchial tubes dilate
- Pupils dilation
- Hair shaft becomes erect

Several of these indicators, by the way, are monitored by the polygraph that is supposed to gauge physiological reactions to lying, which produces stress in most people.

During this activation of ANS systems, the hypothalamus continues to organize a chain reaction of defenses by releasing several stress hormones. The pituitary gland (the master gland at the base of the brain) is signaled to produce ACTH, a stress hormone. ACTH communicates with other glands to make more stress hormones, which then notify the brain stem (responsible for motor movement, among other functions) to alter organ activity. These biochemical reactions further reinforce the physiological processes that lead to increases in heart rate, blood pressure, and so forth. As a result, you now have the physical and mental energy to decide the best course of action and act on it by either fighting back or fleeing that dark alley. (See Figure 4–4.)

Under these conditions of severe stress, humans have been known to perform unusual feats of strength and endurance. For example, stories have been reported of mothers who can lift a car off of their trapped child due to the dramatic increases in energy and strength caused by this flight and fight system.[4] Even under less severe conditions of stress, however, awareness and attention are heightened and physical strength increases.

According to the "suboptimal arousal theory," it is this very system that allows humans and other primates to be conditioned by our environment. For example, when you reach for a cookie as a child and your mother slaps your

---

[4]The drug PCP (phencyclidine) so extremely activates this system that users have been known to gouge their eyes out, jump out of windows, and take several bullets, not only without feeling their effects, but showing superhuman levels of endurance and strength.

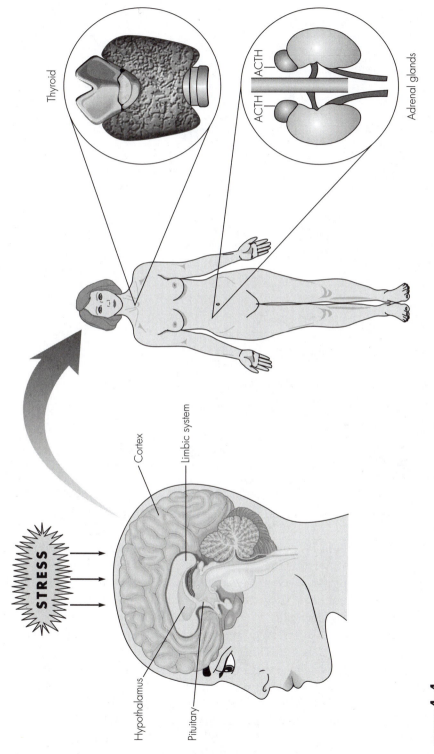

FIGURE 4–4

The hypothalamus coordinates our response to stress by unleashing a flurry of hormonal secretions from the pituitary, thyroid, and adrenal glands. These hormones, in turn, trigger physiological and behavioral reactions that enable us to cope with the stressor. If this biological process is disturbed, our behavior will be disturbed accordingly.

47

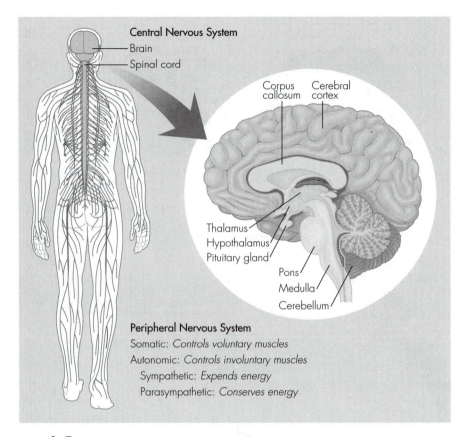

Central Nervous System
Brain
Spinal cord

Corpus   Cerebral
callosum   cortex

Thalamus
Hypothalamus
Pituitary gland
Pons
Medulla
Cerebellum

Peripheral Nervous System
Somatic: *Controls voluntary muscles*
Autonomic: *Controls involuntary muscles*
   Sympathetic: *Expends energy*
   Parasympathetic: *Conserves energy*

FIGURE 4–5

The human nervous system consists of the central nervous system and the peripheral nervous system, each with major subdivisions. The close-up of the brain shows the right hemisphere as seen from the midline.

hand, this stress system is activated to some extent, causing you to feel discomfort and anxiety. Thus, you are deterred from repeating that behavior. The mere threat of punishment becomes uncomfortable enough that you probably won't try again without permission. As adults, most of us have been conditioned effectively enough to know not to steal or harm others simply due to the threat of punishment or negative consequence. This entire criminal justice system is premised on its ability to condition our behavior.

What happens when this "stress" system is hyperactive, that is, when it is too quick to respond or it responds without adequate provocation from the environment? Researchers believe that individuals prone to panic attacks may suffer from a hyperactive ANS that is much too sensitive and causes experiences of panic and fear when the context does not warrant such a reaction. For these individuals, medications that suppress this stress system (also often used in cardiac patients) generally work well to stabilize the ANS. (See Figure 4–5.)

On the other hand, what happens when this system is underactive? What happens when an individual does not experience a sufficient flurry of hormones or physiological activation to produce discomfort? The result can be an underactive CNS and ANS—the individual may not be "conditionable" because, in the absence of physiological and emotional discomfort, they will not respond appropriately to punishments or threats of punishments. Research suggests that such individuals cannot be effectively deterred from crime or high-risk behaviors merely with threats of punishment. As you will see in the box on page 53, the psychopath is characterized by this underactivity of biochemical and physiological responses. In the subsections that follow, indicators of low CNS and ANS arousability, which have been related to aggression and other antisocial behaviors, are discussed: EEG, evoked potentials, skin conductance, and heart rate.

EEG and Evoked Potentials   Physiological markers indicative of central nervous system instability have been repeatedly found in subjects with antisocial behavior, as reflected in electroencephalogram (EEG) differences, and electrodermal (skin), cardiovascular, and other nervous system measures (see Elliott, 1992; Fishbein, 1990; Fishbein et al., 1989b; Hare, 1984; Hare & Schalling, 1978; Raine, 1993; Raine et al., 1997b). In particular, researchers have used the EEG method to identify differences in brain activity between people with behavioral disorders and those without. The EEG uses electrodes placed on top of the scalp to record electrical activity from below the scalp and within the cortex. An EEG recorder can also be used to monitor brain activity when an individual is presented with a stimulus so that the researcher can actually track the brain's response as it travels through various regions to be registered and recognized. The signals received by the EEG recorder during this process are called "evoked potentials," which are usually monitored after either a sound, visual, or tactile stimulus, or a thinking task is presented.

Individuals with a history of drug abuse and those with impulsive aggression tend to show relatively more slow wave activity in their EEG and delays in their evoked potentials (EPs), particularly when presented with an auditory stimulus, as compared to those without these disorders. Given that there are four wave lengths (two slow and two fast), individuals who have a greater amount of the slow waves may not process information as efficiently or effectively; thus, such slowing may be related to cognitive deficits (Begleiter et al., 1987; Fishbein, 1990; Howard, 1986; Pincus & Tucker, 1974; Raine, 1993; Syndulko et al., 1975). Delays in evoked potentials as they travel from the brain stem into the center of the brain to be registered also indicate an inefficiency in information processing. Relatively high levels of EEG slowing and EP delays in these subjects are thought to reflect arrested development of the brain and its function, although such findings lack specificity. These processes are often a function of irregularities in neurotransmitter systems that alter

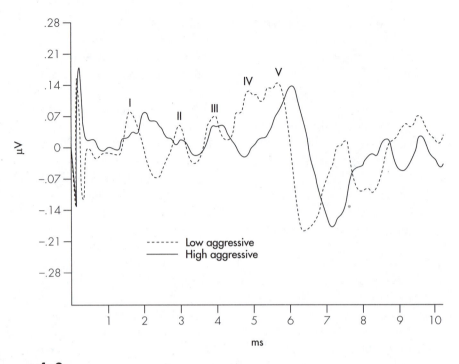

FIGURE**4–6**

When a sound is repeatedly introduced to subjects, the brain processes it in predictable ways from the auditory nerve, through the brainstem and up into higher cortical centers. Electrophysiological recordings of this process are called "evoked potentials" (EPs). Research such as this study have shown that subjects with a significant history of childhood aggression and/or psychopathy process these stimuli less efficiently than those without such a history, showing delays in the brain's response. Along with findings of an increased amount of slow wave activity in the EEG in aggressive subjects, these neurophysiological findings suggest the presence of a developmental lag in this group.

CNS arousal levels and, thus, may contribute to excessive stimulation needs (Raine, 1993). (See Figure 4–6.)

Skin Conductance and Heart Rate   Skin conductance (SC) measures the electrical activity in the skin and reflects the function of part of the nervous system outside of the brain and spinal cord—the peripheral nervous system, which includes the autonomic nervous system. It is also, however, regulated by regions within the CNS. When SC responses to a stimulus are elevated, that means electrical activity within the skin is high. This reaction is a sign of the degree to which an individual is aroused and, therefore, is an indication of emotional state. Polygraphs, used with criminal suspects as an indication of lying, monitors skin conductance as well as other autonomic responses. Theoretically, when an individual is lying, their autonomic nervous system becomes highly activated because most of us have been conditioned not to deceive. Thus, SC, heart rate, and respiration all rise (see Figure 4–7).

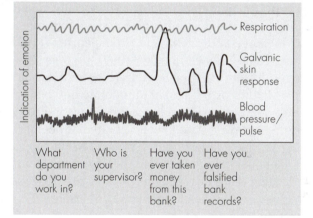

FIGURE**4–7**

The polygraph, a method for detecting nervous arousal, is the basis for the so-called lie detector test. The polygraph operator asks a series of nonthreatening questions to establish baseline readings of the subject's autonomic responses, then asks questions relevant to an investigation. The underlying assumption is that an increase in arousal indicates nervousness, which in turn indicates lying. Unfortunately, a large percentage of innocent people also become nervous and therefore appear to be lying.

Most studies of SC and its relationship to aggressiveness or antisocial be-havior have focused on a subgroup of criminal offenders classified as psycho-pathic, as described later (Hare & Schalling, 1978; see Raine, 1993 for review). Consistently, investigators have reported findings of low SC arousal in this population (Blair et al., 1997). Deficits in measures of SC arousal are believed to be associated with low autonomic arousal levels which are, in turn, related to low emotionality, poor conditionability, lack of empathy and remorse, and ability to lie easily. Put simply, individuals who do not respond to emotional stimuli (e.g., a bloody knife) with an emotional response (e.g., fear) are more difficult to condition by threats of punishment and more likely to seek out high levels of stimulation. For example, most people will show high SC responses when they receive penalties while playing gambling-type games or when words with emotional overtones (e.g., murder, knife, blood as opposed to chair or water) are presented. A subgroup of individuals, however, do not show these emotional responses orchestrated by the autonomic system, and it is this subgroup that are considered to have a greater likelihood of engaging in high-risk and aggressive behaviors.

Low SC responses are indicative of both structural and functional abnormalities in both the autonomic nervous system and the area behind the forehead, the frontal cortex. It is the frontal part of the brain that is responsible for higher intellectual cognitive functions and regulation of emotional responses (Hazzlett et al., 1993; Raine et al., 1991). In psychopathic and aggressive people, such deficits in SC may be outwardly expressed as reduced or inappropriate emotional responses to socially meaningful stimuli. Because both serotonin and dopamine play a regulatory role in the production of skin conductance in the ANS and frontal cortex (Mirkin & Coppen, 1980; Raine et al., 1990; Yamamoto et al., 1990), there is strong speculation that SC deficits result from a central neurotransmitter imbalance.

Heart rate is another expression of autonomic nervous system function that reflects emotional state; thus, a low heart rate is indicative of low ANS arousability. During a resting state, low heart rate has been reliably found in antisocial and aggressive youngsters (see reviews in Raine et al., 1997a and Raine, 1993). A meta-analysis (Raine et al., 1997b) reported an average effect size of 0.53, indicating that low resting heart rates predict conduct disorders to some extent in various childhood samples. Furthermore, Farrington (1987) reported that resting heart rate at age eighteen to nineteen years in a sample of noninstitutionalized males predicted violent offending at age twenty-five in statistically significant ways. These sorts of findings are consistent with the widely tested hypothesis that subjects with antisocial, psychopathic, and repeatedly violent behavior are more likely to be physiologically underaroused and, consequently, seek an unusual amount of stimulation in an advertent attempt to arouse their underaroused nervous systems (see Raine, 1993).

Many of these psychophysiological markers are nonspecific for psychiatric, psychological, or behavioral disorders. In other words, the physiology may contribute to an orientation or predisposition to certain patterns of behavior, but the actual behavioral outcome may be more a function of socio-environmental experiences. Also, the reader should keep in mind that without accurate and consistent diagnosis or measurement of behavior, findings reported become suspect or, at a minimum, less meaningful; each study must be judged individually. Nevertheless, taken together these studies suggest irregularities in arousal level which are consistent with findings of neurotransmitter dysfunction.

4–1 *Psychopathy*

Psychopathy is a syndrome or pattern of behaviors and psychological traits that were characterized by Cleckley (1964) as having the following features:

- Charming
- Appearing intelligent
- Lack of nervousness
- Untruthful
- Insincere
- Lack of remorse or shame
- Inadequately motivated antisocial behavior
- Poor judgment
- Failure to learn from experience
- Pathological egocentricity
- Incapacity for love
- Emotionally flat
- Lack of insight
- Unresponsiveness to relationships

There has been great confusion regarding the concept of psychopathy as opposed to sociopathy and *Antisocial Personality Disorder* (ASPD) (APA:DSM-IV, 1997). Sociopathy is not a psychiatric classification; it is a social construct used often to describe individuals who have no regard for the law or social norms. Sociopaths are simply individuals who break the law, and there are no particular underlying mechanisms to explain their behavior. Often their behavior is described as being a result of a lack of socialization, but the concept of sociopathy has been historically poorly measured and characterized. ASPD, on the other hand, is a personality disorder described in the Diagnostic and Statistical Manual of the American Psychiatric Association (DSM-IV). This diagnosis describes individuals who disobey authority and eventually the law with an early onset of defiant and deviant behavior. While psychopaths also generally fall into the category of ASPD, they are a particular subgroup, believed to differ from others in this category by virtue of deviations in physiological and brain functional measures.

Individuals thought to be psychopathic are not out-of-control, drooling, homicidal maniacs. Quite the contrary, they have been referred

(continued)

to as "reptile-men," "automatons," or "mechanical men" because they appear to lack emotion and empathy for others. They are cool, calm, and collected. They obtain pleasure from risky behaviors, dangerous situations, and thrill seeking. The epitome of a psychopath is a serial murderer (although some serial murderers instead suffer from paranoid schizophrenia) who kills without remorse and achieves a thrill from the process itself. They are also more likely to abuse drugs and alcohol; studies have reported that individuals with either psychopathy or ASPD are more sensitive to the rewarding properties of drugs and less sensitive to their adverse effects.

Psychopaths have been found to differ from nonpsychopaths in several physiological measures. These indices include (a) EEG differences, (b) cognitive and neuropsychological impairment, and (c) electrodermal, cardiovascular, and other nervous system measures (Newman, 1987). In particular, psychopathic individuals have been found to show relatively slower wave activity in their EEG compared with controls, which may be related to differences in cognitive abilities. Relatively high levels of EEG slowing found in psychopathic subjects may reflect a delay in the maturity of the brain. Thus, EEG slowing among individuals who also demonstrate poor regulated behavior and an inability to learn from experience may reflect a developmental delay. EEG slowing among some psychopaths is consistent with findings of hypoaroused autonomic function and other differences in psychophysiologic parameters. Their need for external stimulation may be higher and more difficult to satisfy than in other populations due to a lower level of internal stimulation (see Raine, 1993).

The implications of many decades of research on psychopathy are that affected individuals may not condition the way most of us do. As explained in the previous section, most individuals' behavioral patterns are conditioned by rewards and punishments. When a behavior results in a painful consequence, we are less likely to repeat that behavior. When a behavior results in a pleasurable consequence, that behavior is reinforced and likely repeated. In order to invoke this process, the physiological responses to environmental input that are necessary to produce the experience of stress must be intact. For example, as children, we are taught that when we engaged in behaviors that are forbidden, we would be punished for that behavior. This is the process of behavioral conditioning. The mere threat of a punishment produces the experience of anxiety, which is uncomfortable and avoidable. Having learned in childhood that certain behaviors are considered "wrong," we are not likely to engage in them in adulthood for the same reasons. We are, thus, avoiding a negative consequence—the anxiety produced when doing something we know is wrong. Threats of punishment, and even lying, causes a chain of physiological responses, unleashed by the ANS, that make us feel uncomfortable and anxious, which is why we don't often engage in "wrong" behaviors. Our criminal justice system's notion of deterrence is based on these principles of behavioral conditioning. The problem with psychopaths, however, is that they do not appear to condition through threats of punishment and, therefore, may not be easily deterred using negative sanctions. Research, some of which is mentioned previously, suggests that their ANS is underactive and, consequently, not able to produce the appropriate anxiety responses to environmental input or stressors. Additional research suggests that their ANS may be under-aroused as a result of a disconnect within the CNS between the cortex (the part of the brain responsible for higher intellectual functions) and the limbic system (the region responsible for emotion, mood, memory, and other functions necessary for survival) (see Damasio et al., 1990). Possibly as a result of their relatively low levels of physiological respon-siveness and lack of anxiety, they are notoriously difficult to treat for their antisocial behavior and also for any co-occurring drug abuse disor-ders they develop.

NEUROPSYCHOLOGICAL AND IMAGING STUDIES

Reviews of a large body of research unanimously conclude that impair-ments in cognitive or neuropsychological functions, which involve informa-tion processing, memory, and assessment of environmental cues, are implicated in poor self-regulation of behavior (Buikhuisen, 1987; Hurt & Naglieri, 1992; Kandel & Freed, 1989; Lueger & Gill, 1990; Milner, 1991; Moffitt, 1990, 1993; Moffitt & Lynam, 1994; Pennington & Bennetto, 1993; Seguin et al., 1995). The evidence specifically suggests that various types of antisocial behavior may be characterized by impairments in ability to assess consequences and act on that assessment, as reflected in the personality trait of impulsivity (Barratt & Patton, 1983; Gray, 1983; Gray & Mc-Naughton, 1983; Newman, 1987; Shapiro et al., 1988). These impairments have been associated with brain function abnormalities that affect cognitive abilities. In particular, problems with executive cognitive functions (ECF) have been found in impulsive and aggressive subjects, including problems with attention, concentration, verbal ability, abstract reasoning, problem solving, and programming and planning goal-oriented behaviors (Mirsky & Siegel, 1994). Giancola (1995) has hypothesized that impaired ECF compromises the ability to interpret social cues during interpersonal interactions, which may lead to misperceptions of threat or hostility in conflict situations. ECF impairment may further undermine the ability to think of alternative behaviors that are more socially acceptable and to execute a sequence of responses necessary to avoid aggressive or stressful interactions. Finally, insufficient control by cognitive processes over behavior may permit hostility and negative affective states, and other maladaptive responses (e.g., violence or drug abuse) to dominate (Giancola, 1995).

The prefrontal cortex and its connections beneath the cortex represent the neural structures most involved in ECF, suggesting their involvement in aggressive behavior, impulsivity, and even drug abuse. Evidence indicates that damage to areas of the prefrontal cortex reduces inhibitions and self-concern, causing affected persons to be indifferent to the consequences of their behavior (Damasio et al., 1990). Thus, areas of the prefrontal cortex are thought to regulate social skills (Carlson, 1994; Damasio et al., 1994). Indications of impaired judgment, inability to assess consequences, attention deficits, and inadequately or inappropriately motivated behavior often characterize individuals with histories of both violence and drug abuse (see Farrington, 1995; Giancola, 1995; Giancola et al., 1996). (See Figure 4–8.)

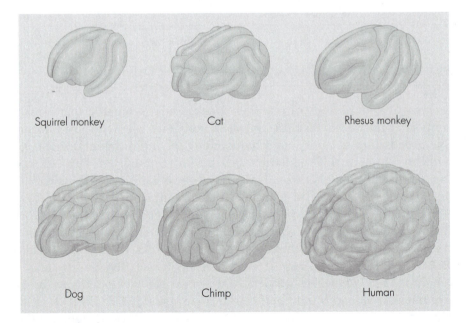

FIGURE 4–8

Species differences in prefrontal cortex.
Note that the prefrontal cortex (shaded area) constitutes a larger proportion of the human brain than of the brains of these other species.

Source: After Fuster, 1989.

4–2 *The Story of Phineas Gage*

On September 13, 1848, a work crew on the Rutland and Burlington Railroad was blasting rock out of a gorge in Cavendish, Vermont. The crew's foreman was Phineas Gage, an energetic and capable man of twenty-five, well liked by his men and respected by his employers. At 4:30 P.M., Gage was charging a hole drilled in the rock, filling it with gunpowder in preparation for blasting. His men worked behind him, loading rock on a nearby platform car. With the powder in place, Gage picked up a specially made tamping iron, a heavy rod three-and-a-half feet long, flattened at its business end and pointed at the other. Gage then instructed his assistants to pour sand in the hole to trap sparks set off by the iron as it descended toward the powder.

A few seconds later, Gage heard a noise behind him and turned slightly to his right. His assistant, also distracted by the sound, hesitated before pouring the sand. Unaware of this, Gage turned back to his task and let the tamping iron drop into the charged hole. As it descended, the tamping iron scraped the shaft and struck a spark, which ignited the powder. Gage's tamping iron shot out like a cannon ball. It struck Gage beneath his left eye, tore through his skull and frontal lobe, and exited near the midline, just above where hair meets forehead. The iron flew fifty feet into the air before landing in the dirt, covered with blood and brains.

Gage's men, who were sure he would not survive, were paralyzed with shock and disbelief when Gage began to speak and was still able to walk. He was rushed to the nearest doctor. The doctor was able to pass the full length of his index finger into the wound without meeting any obstruction in Gage's head.

Over the next several weeks, Gage's progress was slow but steady. But while Gage's physical recuperation was almost complete, his personality had undergone a profound alteration. Gage's physician described his personality transformation as follows: "The equilibrium, or balance, between his intellectual facilities and animal propensities, seems to have been destroyed. He is fitful, irreverent, indulging at times in the grossest profanity (which was not previously his custom), manifesting but little deference for his fellows, impatient of restraint or advice when it conflicts with his desires, at time pertinaciously obstinate, yet capricious and vacillating, devising many plans of future operation which are no

(continued)

sooner arranged than they are abandoned in turn for other appearing more feasible. A child in his intellectual capacity and manifestations, he has the animal passions of a strong man. Previous to his injury he possessed a well-balanced mind and was looked upon by those who knew him as a shrewd, smart businessman, very energetic and persistent in executing all of his plans of operation. In this regard, his mind was radically changed, so decided that his friends and acquaintances said he was 'no longer Gage.'"

Based on the experiences of Phineas Gage and their effects on his personality, temperament, and intellect, neuroscientists began to understand that the damaged area was responsible for social skills, impulse control, forethought, and assessment of consequences in all human beings. This area is the orbitofrontal cortex, within the prefrontal cortex, which has remained the focus of numerous investigations into disregulated and disinhibited behavioral problems, including those involving drug abuse, alcoholism, CDs (Conduct Disorders), and antisocial behaviors. (See Figure 4–9.)

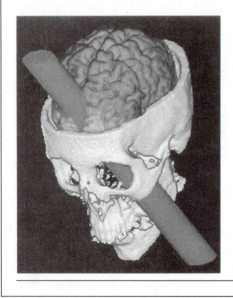

FIGURE 4–9

In the 1990s, researchers used modern technology to reconstruct the path that an iron bar must have taken through the brain of Phineas Gage, who survived this injury in 1848. The damage impaired Gage's judgment and decision making.

Several lines of evidence implicate dysfunction of the prefrontal cortex specifically in violent behavior. For example, head injury affecting the prefrontal cortex has been associated with post-injury violent behavior (see Volavka, 1995). Patients and offender populations with prefrontal lobe damage show increased extraversion, impulsivity, irritability, aggressiveness, and various antisocial behaviors (see Kandel & Freed, 1989). Patients with prefrontal lobe head injuries often exhibit problems in their ability to make rational decisions in personal and social matters, in addition to difficulties in the processing of emotion (Damasio et al., 1994). In brain injured individuals, a functional disconnect between frontal cortical regions and the limbic system may result in impaired impulse control, reasoning, and decision making.

While neuropsychological tests provide some guidance in the search for neural mechanisms in antisocial behavior, they lack the ability to locate the specific regions involved in these functions and behaviors. Also, they tend to measure general neuropsychological function, like IQ and memory, rather than ECF specifically. More recently developed techniques are now able to provide more information on the location of function, however. If we want to fully understand these cognitive processes and their relationship to antisocial behavior, it is necessary to directly measure neural responses in particular brain regions while individuals with and without antisocial behavior perform relevant cognitive tasks. The most promising method is the use of neuroimaging techniques to identify structural differences and functional brain responses to cognitive stimuli that challenge regions thought to be involved in ECF (e.g., via positron emission tomography [PET] or functional magnetic resonance imaging [fMRI]).

In one of the few brain imaging studies examining individuals with persistent aggressive behavior, differences in the metabolism of glucose in a region of the prefrontal cortex was reported (Goyer et al., 1994). PET studies of individuals with disruptive behavioral disorders that often precede impulsive-aggression in adulthood have focused primarily on Attention Deficit Hyperactivity Disorder (ADHD). Zametkin et al. (1990) reported lower levels of global and regional glucose metabolism in areas of the prefrontal cortex and limbic system in ADHD adults than controls without ADHD. In an important study, Raine et al. (1997c) examined forty-one murderers and forty-one age-matched controls using PET and an attention task which produces increases in glucose metabolism in particular brain regions in normal subjects (Buchsbaum et al., 1990). Primary findings were that murderers exhibited reduced glucose metabolism during the task in both sides of the prefrontal cortex, in addition to several other structures. Raine and his colleagues concluded that these murderers have deficits in prefrontal function.

Imaging studies of impulsive and aggressive behavior suffer from one or more shortcomings, including small sample size, technological shortcomings, ambiguity in group assignments, and absence of a cognitive task to activate various brain structures to "localize" cognitive function. Nonetheless, these studies offer provocative information on brain function in impulsive-aggressive individuals and provide the basis for more definitive investigations.

INTERWEAVING ENVIRONMENTAL AND BIOLOGICAL INFLUENCES OVER TIME: DEVELOPMENTAL PROCESSES

Research into the multiple determinants of the risk for antisocial behavior requires a developmental perspective to place into context the fluid interaction between environmental and biological factors described herein. The age of onset for antisocial behaviors is not equally distributed throughout the life span among the population of individuals who exhibit these behaviors. This variability is a direct function of changes over time in biological and behavioral processes that result from ongoing interactions with many different environments (Tarter et al., 1998). For example, family situations, peer interactions, school settings, and work environments are typically not static in an individual's lifetime, and produce measurable changes in biological systems and behavioral outcomes as the individual ages. Epidemiological data provides support for the notion that some external conditions are more important influences at certain points in the life span than others; e.g., maternal influences during childhood, peer influences during adolescence, and the use of drugs with pain-reducing or pleasure-producing properties later in life when stress or pain becomes more prevalent. Thus, there is an essential feedback loop between preexisting traits, behavioral outcomes, and environmental influences which fluctuate throughout the life span and contribute to varying degrees of "risk" or liability for antisocial behavior at any given stage of life (see Elliott, 1994; Farrington, 1995; Kelley et al., 1997; Loeber & LeBlanc, 1991; Loeber & Stouthamer-Loeber, 1998; and Quay, 1987 for reviews).

Ralph Tarter (1998) has employed a developmental approach for understanding the etiology of substance abuse disorder. His developmental model can readily be applied to an understanding of antisocial behaviors in general:

> This perspective emphasizes the influence of cumulative prior experience as the major determinant of the emergence of each successive phenotype. This epigenetic process allows understanding of the etiology of drug abuse in the context of an orderly process in which the outcome is the culmination of an ongoing developmental trajectory concomitant to person-environment interactions. It is important to note, however, that other outcomes (e.g., AIDS, criminality, dementia) can likewise be investigated through continued monitoring of the trajectory across the lifespan. Thus, drug abuse is not necessarily the only or final outcome of interest but instead is commonly intermediary to other negative outcomes. The epigenetic approach enables, therefore, the integration and sequencing of

adverse outcomes associated with drug abuse as well as quantitative analysis of the patterning of other outcomes. (p. 233)

Although Tarter's model addresses the development of drug abuse specifically, the implications are relevant to all complex human behavior. Healthy, normal development is characterized by the mastery of particular developmental tasks, such as cognitive and verbal skills, honesty, understanding rights of possession, respect for authority, independence, and basic trust. Successful development, defined by the mastery of these tasks, is conducive to prosocial behavior and incompatible with antisocial behavior, generally resulting in a well-adjusted social behavioral repertoire. And while there are bases in evidence for the tendency of resultant behavioral patterns to wax and wane over time (dependent upon both physical and psychological stages of development), most assume a predictable pathway, in the absence of any intervention or drastic socio-environmental change.

Antisocial behavior tends to have an early onset and often persists into adolescence and adulthood (Farrington et al., 1990; Loeber & Stouthamer-Loeber, 1998; Patterson et al., 1989), suggesting that it is (1) a developmental trait, and (2) somewhat a function of the inability to incorporate the developmental tasks listed earlier. Early manifestations of high risk for antisocial behavior may include difficult temperament, impulsivity, social adjustment problems, physical fighting, poor academic achievement, distractibility, and, oftentimes, depressed or negative mood. Attention deficit hyperactivity disorder is especially prevalent in early onsetters who progress to more serious criminal offending. These early signs commonly originate in genetic, congenital, and prenatal processes that subsequently interact with contextual factors to further condition the relationship between biology and behavior (see for example, Piquero & Tibbetts, 1999 and Tibbetts & Piquero, 1999). A few of the contextual variables that exacerbate this developmental process, and contribute to a negative feedback loop, include parental rejection, ineffective parenting practices or severe disciplinary responses, child abuse, parental substance abuse, negative peer influences, poverty, and negative feedback from teachers. In short, the child's responses to information from the environment stimulate predictable reactions from the social environment, reinforcing or counteracting the child's reactions, contributing to further changes in reactions from both the social environment and the child: "Each step in this action-reaction sequence puts the antisocial child more at risk for long-term social maladjustment and criminal behavior" (Patterson et al., 1989: 329). Rather than replacing one behavior with another in response to changing socio-environmental conditions, however, behaviors diversify and either strengthen, weaken, or reverse the developmental path over time.

SUMMARY

This chapter provides a detailed, albeit not exhaustive, review of several biological factors that have been associated with propensity to engage in antisocial behavior. From the chemicals circulating throughout our brains and bodies (biochemistry), to the electrical impulses generated from our actions, moods and thoughts (physiology), to the ways in which our brains process information from the environment (neuropsychology), we are each unique and, thus, uniquely predisposed to characteristic behavioral responses and patterns. Recent scientific advances have enabled us to identify those biological factors that are most consistently related to various forms of antisocial behavior, even though much additional work needs to be done to show cause and effect. Nevertheless, it is essential to keep in mind that none of these factors act alone; they are dynamically related to one another. Thus, rarely does one biological condition stand out above the others for its influence on antisocial behavior. Instead, there is more often a constellation of these factors interacting in a fluid manner to influence behavior. And, as the final section of this chapter reminds us, biological factors do not act in a vacuum. Their effects are constantly changing as a function of age and developmental stage within a constantly changing environmental and social context.

The prevention and treatment implications of this approach are significant: given that antisocial behaviors tend to be fairly predictable and potentially understandable, they are a viable target for prevention (Patterson et al., 1989). This research further demands that interventions be designed for and sensitive to variations in significant influences and changes in behavioral and psychological traits that occur during different stages of life. By understanding what underlies and stabilizes antisocial developmental paths, the opportunities for treatment and prevention improve the likelihood of successful alterations of that pathway (Nagin & Farrington, 1992).

The next chapter concentrates on how the social and physical environment directly influence the biological processes discussed so far. There is clear evidence that biological, and even genetic, factors are not static nor unchangeable. Rather, our biology in the form of biochemical and physiological responses and neuropsychological functions are sensitive to environmental input and can be altered to varying degrees. Genetic predispositions to certain traits and behaviors can also be altered through feedback from the environment by changing the way in which genes are expressed. Because our experiences and exposures determine, to great extent, the pathway individuals will tend toward in life, our discussion now turns to external factors that influence biological processes that are believed to underlie antisocial behavior. This chapter is particularly important given that the focus of this text is on behaviors that we would ultimately like to modify–violence, drug abuse and addiction, and psychopathy.

SOCIO-ENVIRONMENTAL CONTEXTS

CHAPTER

5

A developmental approach to studying human behavior helps us to understand how biological and environmental variables interact over the life span. And although both biological and environmental conditions are powerful predictors of antisocial behavior and drug abuse, neither are "causal" in a deterministic sense—they are probabilistic.[5] The intensity and frequency of exposure to negative environmental conditions, and the number and severity of internal risk factors present, determine the degree to which an individual is at risk for behavioral disorders. People who are inherently vulnerable by virtue of their genetic make-up and/or biological constitution, and are exposed to an adverse environment, are at imminently greater risk, particularly when adverse external influences accumulate over time. Theoretically, the presence of an increasing number or severity of these factors can influence the development of antisocial or drug taking behaviors by altering brain function, disengaging coping mechanisms, and compromising ability to formulate and act on rational choices.

Research in neurobiology and behavioral genetics has demonstrated that individuals vary considerably with respect to their biological strengths (protective factors) and weaknesses (risks). Biological weaknesses or vulnerabilities are influential in an individual's risk for antisocial behavior. Rather than acting alone, however, this body of research suggests that these biological conditions operate by setting the stage for how adaptively an individual will respond to personal stressors. A stressful environment is more likely to contribute to some form of psychopathology when it is received by a biological system that is somehow compromised. Thus, although the probability of a pathological response is a function of the number and severity of individual risk factors present, the probability is even greater in the presence of an adverse environment with severe stressors.

---

[5]This is the central tenet of the so-called biosocial approach in criminology.

So far, neurobiological research shows that stress, both internally and externally induced, affects neurological processes and behavioral outcomes during particular phases of development. The environment can contribute to changes in behavior by altering:

- Neurotransmitter responses
- CNS and behavioral activity levels
- Blood flow and glucose metabolic rates in the brain
- Development of connections between brain cells over time
- Aspects of brain function that control both the immune system and psychological responses (psychoneuroimmunology)
- Density of autoreceptors in the brain that affect regulatory capabilities
- Hormonal responses
- Physiological responses and tone

Deviations in these biological processes often underlie many types of behavioral disorders.

Social, economic and physical deprivation, poverty, traumatic stress, family dysfunction, prenatal drug exposures, and other negative childhood experiences and environmental conditions all have a profound impact on brain function. Conversely, brain dysfunction has an impact on environmental or social responses to the individual, compounding the risk for an adverse behavioral outcome. Manifestations of these impacts are measurable in cognitive processes (e.g., attention deficits), behavioral patterns (e.g., conduct disorder), temperamental traits (e.g., impulsivity or sensation-seeking), psychophysiological indices (e.g., EEG or skin conductance), and/or neurochemical aberrations (e.g., serotonin or cortisol). Of relevance here is that these indicators of brain function are now known to be sensitive to improvements in our social environment in ways that may decrease risk for antisocial behavior and drug abuse. Aspects of brain function that are believed to underlie these disorders are both genetically determined and environmentally influenced, thus, their presence can cumulatively alter an individual's developmental pathway to influence later development and behavioral outcomes. More scientific studies are needed to isolate the neurological effects of these factors, providing greater insight into specific brain-environment interactions.

Exposure to a chronic or reoccurring stressor often results in a cumulative effect on biological responses which can impair coping abilities, and poses a formidable risk factor. As a consequence, chronic stress primes the brain for maladaptive responses to the environment, thereby increasing the likelihood of psychopathological or antisocial behavior (Anisman & Zacharko, 1986). Inherent susceptibilities or vulnerabilities help to determine particular behavioral outcomes of that stress, for example, from schizophrenia to depression to violence, while positive attributes of either the individual or the environment can provide some protection from these outcomes. Evidence suggests that particular environmental stressors, in interaction with individual vulnerabilities, present the greatest risk for antisocial behavior. Selected examples of this interaction are highlighted here.

THE PHYSICAL ENVIRONMENT AND ITS STRESSORS

Prenatal Influences

Conditions within the womb where a fetus develops has direct effects on organ function, the anatomy, cognitive ability, intelligence level, psychiatric status, and behavioral patterns (Glover, 1997). The mother's experiences and mental state influence this internal environment and, consequently, play an active role in determining the range of abilities the child will have in interaction with his or her genetic make-up. Her nutritional intake, use of substances, and even stress levels directly affect fetal development. Hundreds of studies document the relationship between suboptimal prenatal conditions and later behavioral and psychological disorders. One particular study (Lou et al., 1994) followed 3,021 women through their pregnancies and compared the 70 most stressed with 50 controls from the sample. Both maternal stress and smoking contributed independently and significantly to premature births, lower birth weight, and small head circumference when adjusted for birth weight. Prenatal stress was also significantly associated with poorer scores on the neonatal neurological examination. Further investigations have begun to examine the specific effects of the prenatal environment on various dimensions and risk factors for behavioral disorders.

The presence of minor physical anomalies is indicative of prenatal trauma or disruption. Minor physical anomalies (MPAs) are abnormalities in the body's structure that occur during pregnancy and reflect a problem in fetal development. Because MPAs are formed during the same process of fetal development that produces the central nervous system, it is reasoned that MPAs are markers of nervous system abnormalities (Fogel et al., 1985). Specifically, certain body features develop at particular times during gestation. A disruption to the fetal environment during that period of time will likely affect the development of those particular features, resulting in visible abnormalities in facial or body form. The visible presence of one or more MPAs provides a clue as to when the insult took place and is reflective of possible damage to portions of the central nervous system that are developing at the same time. A disruption during the first trimester of pregnancy is perhaps most insidious given that all major organs are forming and that the brain is in a critical and vulnerable phase of development. Table 5–1 provides a list of typical MPAs resulting from prenatal trauma.

Several studies have identified multiple MPAs in behavioral and developmental disorders (Pomeroy et al., 1988) associated with antisocial outcomes.

TABLE 5–1	MINOR PHYSICAL ANOMALIES (WALDROP AND HALVERSON, 1971)	
Head circumference out of normal range		Asymmetrical ears
More than one hair whorl		Soft pliable ears
Fine electric hair		No ear lobes
Epicanthus		High steepled palate
Hypertelorism		Furrowed tongue
Malformed ears		Curved fifth finger
Low-set ears		Single palmar crease
Wide gap between first and second toes		Third toe longer than second
Partial syndactalia of toes		

For example, Bell and Waldrop's (1982) review found that high MPA counts in males during the newborn period have shown strong predictive relationships with preschool temperament factors such as short attention span, high activity level, and aggressive-impulsive behavior. For females, high anomaly scores showed relationships with short attention span and inhibited behavior. Fogel et al. (1985) found high MPA counts to be associated with hyperactive behavior in normal and clinical populations of boys, and with inhibited behavior in normal groups of girls. Kandel et al. (1989) tested the hypothesis that MPAs predict adolescent and adult recidivistic violent criminal behavior. The number of MPAs was measured at eleven to thirteen years of age and police records of criminal behavior were ascertained at twenty to twenty-two years of age. Recidivistic violent offenders showed an elevated level of MPAs compared to subjects with one violent offense or subjects with no violent offenses. Mednick and Kandel (1988) further reported that MPAs appear to be strongly related to hyperactivity and later criminal involvement, but only if the offender was reared in an unstable, nonintact family. They concluded that indices of perinatal problems relate to later violent crime, rather than to property crime, and may have as their basis some form of trauma occurring very early in life.

One of the most profound and also preventable contributions to behavioral and psychological disorders during pregnancy is prenatal drug exposure. Animal and human studies indicate that repeated prenatal exposures to drugs of abuse leads to disruptions in normal neurotransmitter function and may enhance development of tolerance and sensitivity to drugs that are taken later in life (Allan et al., 1998; Battaglia et al., 1995; Henry et al., 1995; Howard & Takeda, 1990; Legido, 1997; Slotkin, 1998).

Alcohol   One very profound and direct cause of mental retardation which is entirely preventable is fetal alcohol exposure. Fetal alcohol syndrome (FAS) is easily diagnosable due to the obvious facial deformities and mental retardation that occur in the child after exposure to large quantities of alcohol consumed during the pregnancy. However, subtler forms of FAS can also result from lower or less frequent intake of alcohol which contribute to less obvious physical deformities, making diagnosis more difficult. Rather than profound mental retardation, these cases may present themselves with cognitive deficits, learning disabilities, hyperactivity, and behavioral problems. Individuals so affected are more vulnerable to psychopathology and, in particular, conduct disordered behavior by virtue of the many risk factors they possess (Backon, 1989; Famy et al., 1998; Streissguth et al., 1991).

Damage to the brain from fetal alcohol exposure may increase vulnerability to behavioral disorders specifically by affecting executive cognitive functioning and verbal skills. Also, research suggests that the activity levels of serotonin in the offspring are lower (Guerri, et al. 1998; Gorio et al., 1992; Tajuddin & Druse, 1988), possibly contributing to the development of impulsivity and aggressiveness. Impairments are exhibited in the following forms:

- An inability to calculate the consequences of one's actions
- Difficulty linking cause with effect
- Impaired logic
- Relative lack of remorse
- Memory and learning impairments
- Inappropriate behaviors and impulsivity
- Defects in abstract thought
- Difficulty in following directions

The social consequences of these neuropsychological deficits include poor judgment and gullibility, increased vulnerability to abuse, rejection by peers, frustration and hostility, association with like-peers, and alienation in school. The impairments suffered by FAS victims last a lifetime and frequently remain undiagnosed.

Tobacco   Maternal smoking during pregnancy may increase the risk for later problems in the offspring that are associated with changes in neural structure and functioning, and cognitive deficits in the child. Several studies show a relationship between smoking during pregnancy and outcomes in the offspring that include criminal and antisocial behavior (e.g., Brennan et al., 1999). Mothers who smoke more than half a pack of cigarettes daily during pregnancy were reported to be significantly more likely to have a child with conduct disorder (Wakschlag et al., 1997). A significant effect of maternal smoking on externalizing behavior problems, for example, oppositional, aggressive, and/or overactive behaviors, was also found (Orlebeke et al., 1997). Others have found an association between maternal smoking in pregnancy and delinquency in the offspring during adolescence and early adulthood, although the cause-effect relationship was unclear (Rantakallio et al., 1992).

Maternal smoking during pregnancy has been further associated with attention deficit hyperactivity disorder in their children (Milberger and colleagues, 1996).

The assumption underlying these and other studies is that maternal smoking causes brain damage by reducing oxygen to the fetal brain and by interfering with the development of neurotransmitter and other behavioral regulating systems. This sort of disruption to chemical systems in the brain could contribute to lower cognitive, psychomotor, language, and academic performance, in addition to hyperactivity and attention deficits (Dunn et al., 1997; Milberger et al., 1996, 1997). While particular types of behavioral disorders have been associated with maternal smoking, it is not yet possible to predict the development of a specific disorder. Also, many who are exposed to tobacco in utero are not obviously affected. It is advisable that we also consider alternative explanations which include the fact that both smoking and offending are more prevalent in the lower social strata, implying that some class-linked social factors may be important in this association. And finally, tendencies toward nicotine addiction and other forms of drug abuse have a genetic component. Given that drug abuse and addiction have been significantly associated with offending, it is possible that the link between maternal smoking and offending in the child may reflect a genetic influence, rather than a direct congenital (from the pregnancy) or social influence. Nevertheless, in combination with a disadvantageous environment (e.g., poor parenting or family dysfunction), the effects of maternal smoking during pregnancy on behavioral problems are expected to be stronger.

Cocaine   In some large urban areas, between 10 and 15 percent of all women in their childbearing years are users of cocaine (Giacoia, 1990). This is unfortunate, since cocaine readily crosses the placental barrier and rapidly becomes concentrated in fetal brain tissue. Chronic prenatal exposure decreases activity of certain brain chemicals (e.g., dopamine) and damages their receptors. For example, prenatal cocaine exposure increases release of neurotransmitters such as norepinephrine, to initiate the "stress response" (fight/flight mechanism). These chemicals are also involved in basic neuropsychological functions (e.g., attention, activity levels, and regulation of anxiety and other emotional states). Cocaine further affects blood flow, possibly resulting in oxygen deprivation, cell death, and a decrease in ability to use nutrients. Mothers who use cocaine are also less likely to obtain prenatal care, follow a proper diet, or experience appropriate weight gain. Similarly, most cocaine users also use alcohol, complicating the ability to understand specifically what cocaine is doing, and obviously compounding the problem for the child.

Consequences to the fetus are believed to be many and varied, from seizures to disrupted sleep patterns and irritability (see Mott et al., 1993), although some babies do not show any noticeable effects. Problems with regulating behavior, attention, and activity levels have been reported which are all risk factors for later behavioral problems. Biobehavioral research shows that receptor activity of serotonin, dopamine, and norepinephrine is altered in cocaine-exposed newborns. These changes in receptor activity have been related to developmental delays that may increase risk for negative behavioral outcomes (Battaglia et al., 1995; Legido, 1997; Seidler & Slotkin, 1992; Slotkin, 1998). Also, abnormalities in the EEGs of these newborns indicate that there may be some CNS instability. Fetal weight tends to be lower, length of the body shorter, and head circumference smaller, but lags in the development of these features become more trivial as the infant matures. The following difficulties have also been observed in some exposed children:

- Impairments in cognition, self regulation of behavior and moods
- Hyperexcitability or depression
- Lowered mental and psychomotor developmental scores
- Deficits in context of free play
- A high rate of scattering, batting, and picking up and putting down toys rather than sustained play or curious exploration
- Minimal brain dysfunction and learning disabilities
- Difficulty in concentrating, interacting with other kids, and playing alone
- Impairment in basic attention processes

Nevertheless, there are controversies regarding the effects of prenatal cocaine exposure on offspring behavior, which have not been documented consistently across studies. Also, it is difficult to isolate the effects of cocaine on the fetus when cocaine-abusing mothers so often are polysubstance abusers and consume alcohol.

Effects on the brain from prenatal drug exposures are strongly dependent upon the quality of the home environment. The lifestyle of the parent can complicate outcomes for the developing child (Azuma & Chasnoff, 1993; Brooks-Gunn et al., 1994). Conditions that often exist in the homes of children prenatally exposed to cocaine include a chaotic environment, a lack of appropriate stimulation, lack of parenting skills, a mother with impaired mental functioning by virtue of her addiction, inappropriate developmental modeling, as well as abuse and neglect. The presence of these conditions increases the likelihood of further impairments to intellectual capability and social-ethical behavior.

Maternal Social Conditions

The social environment of a mother during pregnancy may also alter the prenatal biological environment, affecting the behavior of the child. Exposure to high levels of stress during pregnancy can influence how physiological, hormonal, and neurotransmitter systems function in the fetus, possibly affecting risk for behavioral problems (Benes, 1997; McIntosh et al., 1995; Roughton et al., 1998; van Os & Selten, 1998; Ward, 1991). There is some evidence that stress from social experiences during this period can activate genes linked to psychological disorders (Benes, 1997; Kaufer et al., 1998; Smith et al., 1997; Stabenau, 1977; van Os & Selten, 1998). In particular, the gene called "C-fos" may be turned on in the fetus by exposure to both maternal stress and drug abuse (Kaufer et al., 1998; Senba & Ueyama, 1997). Increased C-fos activity is believed to contribute to the development of abnormal neural connections, causing neurons to fire erratically, which may elicit feelings or behaviors that are out-of-context given environmental conditions. As a result, children who experience high levels of stress, hypothetically either in utero or in early life, may become more sensitive to future stressful experiences and exhibit inappropriate emotions associated with mental disorders (Post, 1992).

Perinatal Complications

Perinatal conditions occur between the seventh month of pregnancy to twenty-eight days after birth (Brennan & Mednick, 1997). Complications during this period include prematurity and delivery difficulties such as oxygen loss, infectious disease, prolapsed cord during delivery, irregular heart beat in the child during delivery, and late-stage drug use. These conditions are believed to increase the risk for negative outcomes, particularly aggressive behavior, presumably as a function of the fetal brain damage they can cause. Piquero and Tibbetts provide a thorough overview of research summarizing the relationship between perinatal factors and antisocial behavior (1999), showing support for the relationship (although there are some inconsistencies). Importantly, the most recent studies suggest a strong interactive relationship between the effects of perinatal complications and the social environment on antisocial outcomes. They conclude from their review that "poor or deficient familial and socioeconomic environments may magnify the effects of pre/perinatal complications." Piquero and Tibbetts surmise that perinatal complications may contribute to neuropsychological deficits that impede the socialization process. In the dual presence of neuropsychological impairment and a poor familial environment, characterized by family dysfunction, neglect or abuse, inconsistent parenting, or lack of supervision, the socialization process is further compromised, exponentially increasing risk for an antisocial outcome.

THE SOCIAL ENVIRONMENT AND ITS STRESSORS

The physical and social environment of the mother and her offspring contributes in substantial and necessary ways to brain development and function.

Not only does the growing brain of a child require a certain amount of physical stimulation, there are also strong biological needs for positive social interactions, bonding, and protection against traumatic experiences. For example, children who were not provided with the most basic academic skills (e.g., learning colors or how to spell their names) during the first few years may have difficulty once they enter school and become academically disadvantaged, even though they may be naturally quite bright. More intense stimulation to sensory and cognitive functions may be necessary for these children to develop properly.

Caregiver-Child Social Interactions

The bond between caregiver and child, and the regular sensory contact that comes from this bond, are basic biological needs; even the most basic biological systems depend on the quality of social stimulation early in life. The brain continues to develop neural connections during the first year of life, by which approximately 50 percent of all human learned responses have formed. Between year one and year three, adaptive responses to the environment are formed, including the essential stage called "basic trust." Through attachments to caregivers, infants and children develop a sense of security, self-efficacy, reassurance about the safety of their environment, and successful experiences with others. Children who do not develop basic trust often have attachment disorders, aggressiveness, attention deficits, anxiety, emotional disturbances, and withdrawal. In the absence of adequate levels of early social stimulation, children lack the foundation to deal with the rigors of daily life and its stressors. Thus, even in the presence of prenatal trauma or perinatal complications, manipulations of the environment can minimize biological risks or disadvantages to alter outcomes.

An example highlighting the importance of adequate caregiver-child interactions in the child's behavior is found in reports on maternal depression. Studies have shown that development is influenced by infants' attachment relationship primarily with the mother (see Goodman & Gotlib, 1999). Mothers who interact infrequently, with less intensity, inconsistently, or with relative unresponsiveness compromise a stable attachment relationship. Studies suggest that, as a result, children manifest various disturbances in affect and mood, cognitive ability, sociability, and coping responses (Allan et al., 1998; Cicchetti et al., 1997; Goodman & Gotlib, 1999). The specific risks for behavioral disorders in the child may be a function of inheritance, a predisposition to problems with regulatory processes in the brain, exposure to negative maternal orientations, and/or the stressful environment (Goodman & Gotlib, 1999). Long-term effects of disturbed mother-child interactions on infant development may be affected by changes in the function of serotonin and norepinephrine systems (Rosenblum & Andrews, 1994).

Environmental Stimulation Needs

Physical and sensory stimulation, from touch to visual explorations of the environment, are essential to develop and maintain proper brain function (Kuhn & Schanberg, 1998). The brain experiences crucial periods when cells must be stimulated adequately to develop vision, language, smell, muscle control, and reasoning ability. Neural connections not supported by the external environment shrink and may die. Animal and human babies who are stimulus deprived are less responsive to their environments and if the condition is chronic, learning impairments, a thinner cortex, inadequate neurotransmitter activity, less dense connections between neurons, and increased incidence of premature aging can occur (Holsboer, 1989; Kempermann et al., 1998; Kuhn & Schanberg, 1998; McEwen, 1997; Stokes, 1995). As a result, coping skills under stressful conditions may be impaired throughout life in affected individuals. One of the most extreme examples of such deprivation is in substandard orphanages where infants lack routine caregiver interactions, both social and sensory; mental retardation and even physical deformities may result in the absence of genetic abnormalities.

Thus, touch has biological value to maintain normal growth and development. Premature animals (Meaney & Aitken, 1985; Meaney et al., 1991) and human babies (Kuhn & Schanberg, 1998) who are touched frequently gain more weight, are more active and alert, and show more brain growth. Not being touched often enough is associated with enzyme deficiencies in the brain and body. For example, "psychosocial dwarfism" is a syndrome caused by a lack of environmental stimulation in an infant leading to too little stimulation of the hypothalamus which regulates the release of growth hormone (Albanese et al., 1994; Voss et al., 1998). As a result, growth is stunted and can be permanent if not reversed at an early age. Because the hypothalamus also regulates many aspects of both survival and emotional responses, underactivity in the hypothalamus due to stimulus deprivation can affect behavior and emotions.

Under conditions of sensory deprivation, individuals tend to seek stimulation the brain requires for proper functioning. The reticular activating system (RAS) is made of fibers that connect the lower centers of the brain with higher cortical centers. The RAS activates the brain in response to information from the environment, enabling people to become aware of and react to that input. When stimulation from the environment is inadequate, due either to sensory deprived conditions or physiological deficiencies within the RAS, the tendency to seek stimulation elsewhere increases. As a child, stimulation needs are primarily physical, often resulting in distractibility, constant motion, inability to sit still, and excessive physical contact with others, as seen in hyperactivity.[6] As the child matures, however, high stimulation needs may be met in

---

[6]Hypoarousal within the RAS has been associated with hyperactivity which may help to explain why the administration of a stimulant, Ritalin, helps to calm and focus a hyperactive child. Their unusual need for external stimulation is counterbalanced when the RAS is receiving proper amounts of internal stimulation.

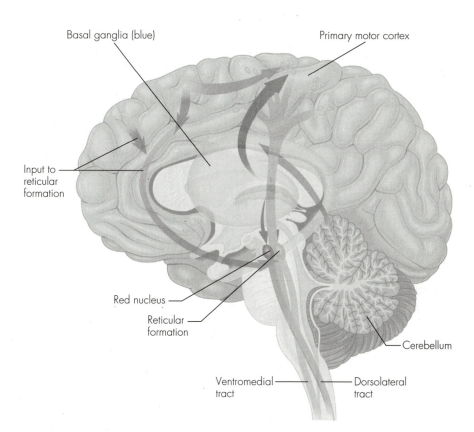

Basal ganglia (blue)

Primary motor cortex

Input to
reticular
formation

Red nucleus

Reticular
formation

Cerebellum

Ventromedial
tract

Dorsolateral
tract

FIGURE 5–1

The major motor areas of the mammalian central nervous system.
The cerebral cortex, especially the primary motor cortex, sends axons directly to the medulla
and spinal cord. So do the red nucleus, reticular formation, and other brain-stem areas. The
medulla and spinal cord control all muscle movements. The basal ganglia and cerebellum
influence movement indirectly through their communication back and forth with the cerebral
cortex and brain stem.

more sophisticated ways by risk taking, novelty seeking, drug use, and other
excessive behaviors. Hypothetically, therefore, even in the absence of a genetic or biological deficit in CNS arousal levels, environmental stimulus deprivation may simulate a condition such as hyperactivity or sensation-seeking
by creating a deficiency state, resulting in increased needs for external stimulation (see Figure 5–1).

In sum, too little stimulation from the environment early in life has been
associated with the development of behavioral disorders, from aggressive
behaviors to depression (Agid et al., 1999; Kuhn & Schanberg, 1998; Post
& Weiss, 1997; Siegel et al., 1993). Underlying mechanisms for this relationship are not yet well understood, although it is likely that the development
of behavioral disorders is a function of cognitive deficits, hormonal and

neurotransmitter irregularities, and other biological effects of deprivation. The particular behavioral disorder that emerges in response to stimulus deprivation, however, is more likely a result of genetic predisposition.

Child Abuse and Other Traumatic Experiences

Child abuse plays a distinct and significant role in the risk for behavioral disorders due to the social and psychological trauma it causes (Maxfield & Widom, 1996). What is less well known, however, is the impact of child abuse on the developing brain which may influence the behavioral response. Child abuse has been associated with alterations in neurotransmitter activity (e.g., serotonin) and stress hormone levels, including cortisol (Kaufman et al., 1997; Lemieux & Coe, 1995; Lewis, 1992). In general, poor parenting has been related to low serotonin levels in the child (Pine et al., 1996, 1997). Furthermore, fewer neural connections, CNS instability (as reflected in EEG abnormalities), and abnormalities in brain development have been reported in individuals with a history of child abuse (Ito et al., 1993, 1998; Shin et al., 1997; Stein et al., 1997b; Teicher et al., 1997). These findings may help to explain the higher incidence of developmental delays and behavioral disorders in this population.

Sexual abuse during childhood has been linked to negative physiological changes that can affect childhood development. In particular, abnormalities in hormone systems and in development during puberty have been found (De Bellis et al., 1994; Stein et al., 1997a). Subgroups of sexually abused girls tend to mature earlier, have different hormonal reactions and possibly develop impaired immune functioning compared to control girls (De Bellis et al., 1996). Higher levels of certain neurotransmitters were noted in abused girls relative to controls. Excessive levels of these particular neurotransmitters and hormones activate stress mechanisms and cause the nervous system to become highly aroused, thus leading to sleep disorders, nervousness and anxiety. Findings suggest that the "fight and flight response" is disturbed in sexually abused girls and other parts of this system attempt to compensate for the abnormality by eventually decreasing cortisol levels, leaving the girls less able to cope with stress. Such disregulation has been linked to depression in other studies of adults (Dinan, 1996).

An unusual level of brain cell death can occur due to high levels of hormone release in response to child abuse and other traumatic childhood events (McEwen, 1997; McEwen et al., 1995; Sapolsky et al., 1996; Smith, 1996; Uno et al., 1994). As a result, chronic stress can lead to learning and memory disabilities by the damage stress hormones cause in brain structures responsible for memory, mood, and other functions. Later in life, the stress associated with traumatic events has been associated with lower social rank, self esteem, and competency in animals and humans (De Goeij et al., 1992; Gust et al.,

1991; Higley et al., 1991; Kraemer et al., 1989; Oates et al., 1985; Sapolsky, 1989; Sapolsky & Mott, 1987; Virgin & Sapolsky, 1997). Irregularities in levels of stress and sex hormones, cholesterol, and immune system function have all been linked to previous stress and present social rank. There is speculation, however, that high quality parenting can minimize problems associated with abnormal levels of neurotransmitter and hormonal activity, regardless of whether the deficit was a function of genetics, environment, or a combination thereof (Field et al., 1998).

Relationships between Prenatal Conditions and Parenting

Babies exposed to prenatal or perinatal disturbances, or predisposed to a difficult temperament, are often more troublesome to care for. While some prenatally or genetically disadvantaged babies sleep excessively, others are more volatile and temperamental, cry more frequently, do not develop normal sleep or eating patterns, have colic, and are difficult to soothe. Furthermore, delays in brain development and greater physical needs are often coupled with a lack of appropriate stimulation from their caretakers, particularly in cases when the mother is a drug abuser, a teenager, or unusually stressed or anxious (McIntosh et al., 1995; Ward, 1991); all conditions are associated with poor prenatal care, drug exposure, and pre/perinatal complications. As a result, these more "difficult" children commonly provoke harsher responses from their caretakers who may not have the psychological or physical resources to cope with their baby's special problems and needs. Once the relationship between the caretaker and child is strained, the risk for abuse and/or neglect is much greater. For example, adopted children at genetic risk by virtue of their biological mother's antisocial behavior were more likely to receive negative parenting (O'Connor et al., 1998b). Thus, in a developmental sense, these children enter the world disadvantaged and, subsequently, experience harsh, inconsistent, or inadequate parenting (O'Connor et al., 1998a, 1998b). Upon entering school, their difficulties are compounded and risk for behavioral disorders heightened when they exhibit learning disabilities, failure in school, social isolation, and further parental rejection (Moffitt, 1993; Moffitt et al., 1993).

Trauma During Adolescence and Adulthood

Traumatic experiences at any point in life can alter brain function. Studies report changes in neurotransmitter activity and metabolism as a consequence of trauma. Interestingly, separation from the mother and social isolation have been shown to increase vulnerability to drug abuse due to the changes they produce in DNA synthesis, hormone responses, and neurotransmitter systems (Kuhn & Schanberg, 1998; Phillips et al., 1997; Piazza & Le Moal, 1996,

1998). Post-Traumatic Stress Disorder (PTSD), a psychiatric disorder caused by severe trauma, is also associated with low levels of serotonin activity and other neurotransmitters (Beckham et al., 1997; Fichtner et al., 1995; Kaufer et al., 1998). There is further evidence that severe stress during adolescence can damage coping responses by disrupting neurotransmitter and hormonal systems (Gerra, 1998; Ryan et al., 1998). Parental divorce, for example, has been associated with abnormal hormonal changes in adolescents (Gerra et al., 1998). Parental divorce can have serious psychological and behavioral consequences during childhood, including problems in peer relationships and a high incidence of aggressive behavior and alcohol consumption. These studies suggest that resulting disorders may be partially due to changes in the release of hormones in the brain induced by the stress of the parental divorce, reducing adaptation to stress in the adolescent. Fortunately, several factors offer some protection from these deleterious conditions, including good quality of the home life, relationships with others, and intimate bonds.

Evidently, exposure to highly stressful and/or novel situations may increase sensitivity of the dopamine reward system (primarily in the limbic system), the same system involved in the rewarding effects of drugs of abuse (Bardo et al., 1996; Cools & Gingras, 1998; Horger & Roth, 1996). Recent studies shed light on individual differences in drug seeking behavior by suggesting that environmental stress may heighten sensitivity of this system, thereby increasing susceptibility to abuse and addiction (Phillips et al., 1997; Piazza & Le Moal, 1996, 1998). Stress can switch genes on or off at the "wrong" times, leading to the development of abnormal networks of brain cell connections which can result in, for example, unusually high levels of stress hormones. When levels of stress hormones are excessive, their presence increases sensitivity of dopamine neurons to drugs, further compounding the risk for drug abuse (see Figure 5–2).

Damage to key brain structures has also been associated with stress and is thought to contribute to irregularities in brain function similar to those that have been related to predisposition to both drug abuse and impulsive-aggressive behavior. The consequences of this sort of damage may include learning deficits, mood disturbances, drug abuse, tension, depression, and an inability to cope with external stressors, which all increase risk for behavioral disorders.

Observing Violence: The Impact of Television Violence

Violence depicted on television these days is both more frequent and severe than in past decades. This dramatic increase in media violence has generated some controversy about whether or not children exposed to violence on television are at increased risk for "acting out" or "externalizing" behaviors. While most studies view this relationship as a result of modeling and

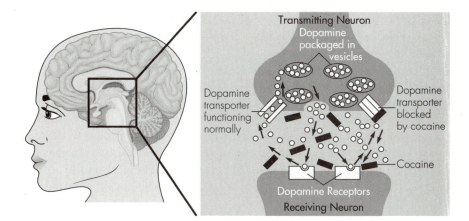

FIGURE 5–2

Dopamine is synthesized in the nerve terminal and packaged in vesicles. For neurotransmission, the vesicle fuses with the membrane and releases dopamine. The dopamine molecules can then bind to a dopamine receptor to exert its effect. After the dopamine binds, it comes off the receptor and is removed from the synaptic cleft by uptake pumps (also proteins) that reside on the terminal (arrows show the direction of movement). This process is important because it ensures that not too much dopamine remains in the synaptic cleft at any one time. When too much dopamine does remain in the synapse, the affected part of brain experiences an excessive amount of excitation, as with the introduction of cocaine. By blocking the reuptake of dopamine back into the sending cell, cocaine causes dopamine to continue to excite the receiving cell much longer than under normal conditions.

social learning, there is also evidence that observing violence may alter the same physiological responses that are related to aggression. Heightened emotional reactions of children to violence on television, as measured by skin conductance, stress hormones, heart rate, and aggressive behaviors, have been reported (Carruthers & Taggart, 1973; Osborn & Endsley, 1971). Significant increases in heart rate have also been associated with viewing violence on television (Groer & Howell, 1990). A stronger skin conductance response to violent shows was found regardless of whether the violence actually occurred or was implied by the situation (Kalamas & Gruber, 1998). Highly violent videotapes elicited more aggressive thoughts than did a less violent tape (Bushman & Geen, 1990). In a second experiment, these investigators found aggressive thoughts increased with the level of violence in the videotape, and physical assaultiveness moderated that effect. Also, hostility and blood pressure were higher in response to the most violent video. These findings and others indicate that stress and emotional systems have been activated in response to viewing TV violence. Activation of these systems likely elicits more acting out behaviors in children with preexisting vulnerability to aggressive behaviors by virtue of their arousability than more "prosocial" children.

SUMMARY

In short, it is clear that the social and physical environment influences our biology and even the expression of genetic traits in direct and measurable ways. When environmental influences are less than adequate or actually harmful to proper functioning of the brain, the result is an increase in risk for various behavioral disorders. For individuals who are unusually vulnerable to these influences (i.e., they possess a multitude of risk factors), these exposures may translate into a greater risk for antisocial behaviors, particularly in the absence of protective influences. On the other hand, it is also clear that manipulating environmental factors in advantageous ways can alter this course and minimize risks in all individuals.

In the following chapter, the shortcomings and controversies surrounding biobehavioral perspectives in criminology are discussed. All research techniques have their weaknesses, and the biobehavioral sciences are no exception. Particular attention is paid to research designs, testing instruments, and interpretations that are specific to the study of genetic and biological contributions to antisocial behavior. Biological approaches to the study of crime have also contributed to quite a bit of controversy over the years given the social, legal, ethical, political, and philosophical issues that arise as a result of the presumed implications of this research. Accordingly, the next chapter is devoted to the "negatives."

THE NEGATIVES: SHORTCOMINGS AND CONTROVERSIES

CHAPTER

6

All fields of research are characterized by shortcomings and controversies, but some are uniquely targeted toward certain disciplines. Shortcomings refer to flaws in the research design, problems with the methods used to measure variables, inappropriate or improperly selected subject population, and misinterpretation of the findings. Controversies that arise from the type of research that is being done or from the way it is conducted usually revolve around social, legal, ethical, or political implications of the results. Both of these negatives need to be addressed before proceeding to do the work, particularly in criminology where the results can directly affect people's lives.

Many of the "negatives" presented in this chapter characterize types of studies of human behavior and misbehavior in general. But several issues have arisen in response to biobehavioral research specifically as a function of attempts to apply genetic and biological tools to the study of criminal behavior. Difficulties in definitions, the use of measurement tools, and interpretations often surface when collaborations are forged across disciplines that are unfamiliar with the techniques, limitations, and research nuances of others. And for reasons that are explained in the following sections, there are both philosophical and scientific obstacles to understanding the roots of crime and criminality.

LIMITATIONS IN RESEARCH METHODS

Research findings from various behavioral sciences that are relevant to the criminologist must first be evaluated in the context of the conceptual framework and the extent to which it fits with frameworks currently used in criminology. The integrity of a study's findings is limited by the concepts chosen, how they are defined, and the relationships between them that are hypothesized and measured—these activities are the ingredients for a conceptual framework. Interpretations of findings that go beyond this frame-work are not considered valid and may be simply speculation or extrapolation; in other words, someone cannot make conclusions about concepts or relation-ships that were not directly studied.

One example related to the concepts selected for study involves the defi-nition that is assigned to the behavior under study. In both criminology and the biobehavioral sciences, concepts often used to study criminal behavior vary widely between studies. Even when the same concept is chosen, it may be defined in different ways or different methods to measure it may be em-ployed. Let's take aggression, for example. Are we really talking about aggres-sive behavior when an individual is given a survey that asks questions about negative or hostile attitudes? Probably not. Attitudes and behaviors do not re-flect the same concept. Thus, it is critical that researchers recognize these dif-ferences and do not report that aggressive behavior is related to some biological trait, when in reality, only attitudes were measured.

Another quick example of how a study's conceptual framework limits in-terpretations involves studies of animals, which provide significant direction for human research. While there are many similarities between monkeys and people, there are certainly at least as many differences! So a researcher interested in identifying the effects of change in a monkey's social environ-ment on serotonin levels, for example, cannot extrapolate those findings to humans.

There are additional limitations generated by the designs and methods used. The design must be appropriate to study the relationships that are hy-pothesized to exist, and the instruments (e.g., survey, behavioral tasks, etc.) employed to measure the variables must yield data that directly describe the concepts, a process called operationalization. While these sorts of shortcom-ings are seen in all studies across all disciplines, certain types of weaknesses tend to characterize some fields more than others. This chapter examines some of the weaknesses often cited in the biobehavioral sciences specifically as they are applied to the study of crime, violence, and drug abuse.

Problems with Defining Concepts

When researchers from any discipline, including criminology, attempt to study criminal behavior, definitional problems often arise. But when investigators from other fields study criminal behavior, they may be even more unaware of the difficulties in defining the behaviors they intend to study. Biobehavioral researchers are frequently not familiar with the operation of the CJS, the plea bargaining process, the diversity of the subject population, and the nature of criminal behavior. The CJS is responsible for "criminalizing" certain behav-iors, all of which are illegal by virtue of the label society gives them. But they vary dramatically with respect to the degree of severity, harm to others, and level of dysfunction they cause within the context of the social setting.[7] In short, not all so-called criminal behaviors are equally dysfunctional, irrational, unethical, or harmful. Focusing on criminal behaviors and crime, then, may really be more about the behavior of the CJS system than of the offender. The plea bargaining process further contributes to this confusion as most offenders have the opportunity to "plea down" their charges. In these common cases, official records of their misconduct may not reflect actual behaviors engaged in during the crime. For example, someone arrested on homicide charges may instead be convicted of involuntary manslaughter. Or even more misleading, violent charges are sometimes reduced, resulting in convictions for nonviolent crimes. So it becomes unclear whether the researcher is studying violent or nonviolent offenders. It is critical that biobehavioral researchers become familiar with the unique properties of criminal offenders and the CJS in order to study them reliably and validly.

Compounding the study of the dependent variable further is the reality that offenders are not a homogeneous group, even within "crime categories." They vary tremendously with respect to behavioral predispositions and histories, family functioning, social experiences, personality and temperamental traits, genetic constitutions, and so forth. Examining the type of crime as the dependent variable completely ignores the diversity of behaviors and relevant traits that may act as contributors, aggravators, or triggers of the criminal behavior.

As a result of unfamiliarity with this population and the system, many investigators choose to focus on crime, criminal behavior, delinquency, violence, and other concepts that are, in large part, socially constructed and a function of the political climate. In other words, use of these concepts as dependent variables ignores the substantial contribution of social institutions and cultural norms to their definitions and to whom they are applied. And in this regard, it ignores the fact that definitions and their applications change over time in response to political movements, cultural events, and large-scale opinion shifts which have nothing to do with behavioral actualities. As suggested in the next section, it is critical that studies concentrate on behavioral phenotypes that can be more reliably measured, can potentially be independently validated, and are not complicated by ever-changing social and systemic processes. Researchers are increasingly recognizing these shortcomings and altering their designs to include behaviors and traits, whose definitions are less constructed by social forces, for example, impulsivity, aggressiveness, sensation-seeking, and anxiety.

Related to these definitional problems, very different conceptual and methodological principles are applied across studies, which makes it difficult

---

[7]Some social settings are more challenging than others and more likely to lead to criminal behaviors for survival purposes—they may not be actually maladaptive or dysfunctional.

to compare and contrast findings. Concepts such as psychopathy, antisocial personality, aggression, criminal behavior, and so on, are not consistently defined and measured in various studies. While one investigator uses criteria for psychopathy to define antisocial behavior, another may use the DSM-IV (APA, 1997) criteria for Antisocial Personality Disorder. While one study may use the Barratt Impulsiveness Scale to measure impulsivity, another study may use the Eysenck Scale or a behavioral measure. Are they measuring the same construct so that we can compare results across studies? The answer to this question is not always clear.

Boundaries for biological measures are also not uniformly identified or operationalized. For example, EEG studies employ different measures of brain activity and different types of stimuli (e.g., auditory or visual) to elicit certain brain responses. Or in the case of serotonin, some studies increase the activity of serotonin and then examine hormone responses, while others may measure serotonin in whole blood. These two techniques do not produce similar measures and must be differently interpreted; one measures serotonin outside the brain and the other inside the brain. Another common example of inconsistency in research methods relates to the role of cognitive variables. Studies employ such a variety of tasks to measure cognition that the measures and interpretations often do not relate to one another; they measure different cognitive processes altogether. Overall, measurement instruments differ among studies and interpretations of findings are variable.

Problems with Generalizability and Representativeness of Samples

Studies of incarcerated populations present obvious problems regarding the generalizability of findings, the extent to which findings describe similar populations that were not directly studied. In these studies, any observed effect or correlation may be due to the effects of institutionalization rather than to the variable(s) of interest. Many studies that used institutionalized offenders as subjects did not attempt to measure or control for prison conditions and influences. We know, for example, that imprisonment can worsen behavioral problems and possibly further impair cognitive functions. So the question becomes: which came first, the impairment or the imprisonment?

Also, prisoners are a selective group, and thus their study does not include individuals outside that population who also exhibit the trait of interest. Many offenders have their charges reduced through plea bargaining, as mentioned earlier. When studying only prisoners, there is no way to document what their crimes may have, in actuality, involved. And what about individuals who engage in the same behaviors but do not get caught or are never incarcerated? The important differences between prisoners and other offenders need to be identified.

Many forms of bias in selecting subjects are also evident in some studies. For example, several studies that focused on criminal offenders ignored pervasive illegal and/or maladaptive behaviors in undetected samples. There is a strong possibility that apprehended or incarcerated subjects differ from those who avoid detection in terms of their characteristics and the impact of criminal justice procedures.

Lack of Proper Control Groups

The use of control subjects is, at times, either neglected or inappropriate. A viable comparison group, which is similar to the target group in demographics, risk status, and other relevant features, is essential in scientific research. A control group tells us (1) whether characteristics of the offenders are unique to that group, (2) the extent to which they differ from the general population, and/or (3) whether changes that occur over time in the target group were in response to an intervention or might have occurred due to other factors. Use of control subjects who are not matched to the target subjects with respect to demographic characteristics or other relevant factors obscure the findings and make it impossible to truly compare groups.

The inclusion of subjects with other types of behavioral disorders (e.g., depression, schizophrenia, homelessness, or head injury) are used all too often as comparison subjects. Imagine that a researcher intends to assess the incidence of neurological defects in a group of violent offenders, and the control group includes nonviolent offenders that are similar demographically. If the control group includes subjects with depression, schizophrenia, or head injury, for example, neurological defects may be overly represented in that group, even though their manifestations may be different. It is best when both target and control subjects are free from psychiatric and other biological disorders and differ only with respect to the presence or absence of violent behavior or other outcome measure of interest.

Unreliable Assessment Tools

Confidence in our data and findings comes from knowing that the tools we used to measure relevant variables are valid and reliable. Some instruments give us more confidence than others. Surveys, including questionnaires and interviews, are notoriously unreliable. They are prone to errors in judgment, memory, and truthfulness. On the other hand, they can be used with some acceptable degree of confidence if other measures supplement them; for example, including official reports and surveys together enables us to compare results from each measure and use them to corroborate each other. Even better is the use of behavioral tests, whenever possible. These tests actually simulate a real-world situation and challenge the subject to behave in response to the task at hand. In some cases, the individual is provoked and their tendency to react aggressively is measured. Other tasks may simulate a gambling card game where the individual is told to make as much play money as possible by finding the best strategy, which means avoiding decks that lead to larger penalties. Individuals who continually select decks that yield large rewards but even larger penalties are considered to have poor decision-making ability and impulsivity. These direct sorts of measures of behavior yield more reliable data than surveys.

Several additional points of caution are particularly relevant to interpretation of studies of psychopathic subjects. The widespread use of self-report and retrospective data is problematic generally, but additional problems arise when these data sources are used to examine offenders, a population notorious for falsifying reports. Psychopaths, who are depicted as crafty deceivers, offer especially unreliable data. Yet, self-report measures are frequently used to select and categorize subjects in all areas of criminology. Not all criminals are psychopaths and vice versa. Moreover, psychological, behavioral, and physiological traits characterizing psychopathy occur along a continuum; psychopathy is not an either-or phenomenon. Thus, both personality traits and actual behaviors must be carefully assessed before assigning subjects to groups. This is true not only for psychopathy, but for many of the behavioral dimensions studied in criminology.

Last, the terminology used to describe individuals exhibiting psychopathic behavior is often inexact, confusing, and inconsistent (Blackburn, 1988). The literature suggests that psychopaths do not form a homogeneous group (Eysenck, 1977; Hare & Schalling, 1978; Raine, 1988). At least two types of psychopaths have been identified that may be more or less prone to criminal activity: primary psychopaths, who are relatively unemotional, and secondary psychopaths, who have high levels of trait anxiety (Blackburn, 1986). It is to be expected that psychopathy with and without anxiety will be characterized by quite distinct physiological conditions and measurable features. Accordingly, reports of psychobiological differences between psychopaths and "normals" have disagreed depending on the definitions and selection criteria used (Devonshire et al., 1988). For these reasons, it is critical that assessment tools rely not only on self-report and paper-and-pencil measures, but that they use standardized criteria, provocative behavioral measures, and an integrated set of variables.

Overreliance on Animal Models

Although the use of animal models to provide direction and *a priori* hypotheses for human studies is critical, one cannot extrapolate from findings in animals to behavior in humans. Many of us do cite a variety of animal studies to provide support for a relationship that is being proposed between various biological markers and dimensions of antisocial behavior, but they are only informative, not definitive. Studies of serotonin activity levels exemplify the proper use of animal models for designing human studies. Early findings showed that serotonin levels were lower in animals with excessively aggressive behavior, and also established that serotonin activity is exquisitely sensitive to environmental and social influences. Using the designs and methods from these animal studies, researchers began to examine human populations with various forms of psychopathology to determine whether these findings translated from monkeys to humans. They did, and the relationship between serotonin, depression, anxiety, impulsivity, and aggressiveness is one of the most reliably established links in psychiatric research. Other areas of research have not been quite so accommodating and we must be careful not to extrapolate from rats and monkeys to humans. Research on testosterone's role in aggression is one particular case in point; while several animal studies show significant effects, human studies have been a bit more inconsistent.

Narrowly Focused Research Parameters

Finally, the majority of so-called multidisciplinary studies have examined only a few variables in isolation, without accounting for interactive effects between biological and socio-environmental conditions. A truly collaborative research project, examining an extensive data set and incorporating the sophisticated methodological and statistical techniques of sociologists, holds the promise of yielding more informative results regarding the nature of bio-socioenvironmental influences on antisocial behavior. (See Mednick et al., 1987, for an additional critique of biological approaches to the study of criminal behavior.)

Biological techniques provide a set of tools for dissecting broadly defined psychological and behavioral concepts like attention deficits, impulsivity, and aggression, and may provide a reality check against too much speculation and theory building (Evenden, 1999). Nevertheless, as we have seen, these techniques have their limitations. There are obvious problems in the way biological techniques can be applied to human subjects, and sometimes neurobiological theories of psychological or psychiatric phenomena lack good support from experimental data and/or animal models. Also, not many biological scientists have adequate knowledge of the unique dimensions, characteristics, and issues that surround studies of criminal offenders. On the other hand, the development of knowledge in the biological sciences is driven by a different set of processes than that in behavioral sciences, and thus there are strong possibilities for progress through cross-fertilization.

RECOMMENDATIONS FOR IMPROVED RESEARCH DESIGNS

Barratt et al., (2000) persuasively argues that there is a profound need for a *neutral interdisciplinary model* for studies on aggression and other correlates of criminal behavior. Development of such a model is critical for effective communication with other behavioral researchers and an understanding of interactions and relative contributions of social and biological factors. Foremost among the steps necessary to achieve this goal is the creation of adequate and accurate assessments of behavioral phenotypes under study. Controversies over measurement techniques and the behaviors of interest are abundant in human research. For social scientists who study antisocial behavior, the controversy often revolves around whether we are actually studying behavior of the individual, the criminal justice system, or society-at-large. For biological scientists, the question is whether we are measuring the behavioral phenotype, the underlying biological response, or the stimulus. An interdisciplinary model would potentially lead to agreed-upon techniques that enable investigators to examine all of these interacting variables with clear definition of what is being studied and what role each one plays in a total social, psychological, and biological environment.

In order to create a neutral model for understanding antisocial behavior, identification of the appropriate target behaviors for study is critical. Emphasis should be placed on the phenotypes or components of antisocial behavior that are measurable, stable, and consistent across cultures, such as aggression, impulsivity, or negative affect. The focus should not be on "crime," per se, which is a legal abstraction, not a behavioral reality. Crime, in many cases, is secondary to these and other underlying problems that remain unattended when left unstudied.

Tarter et al., (1998) outlined several research strategies using animal models to address questions pertaining to liability for drug abuse that can be adopted for studies of human antisocial behaviors. The few recommendations delineated below extend from these approaches for application in human research. These strategies can be viewed as "next steps" needed to estimate relative and interactive influences of biological and social factors, determine the extent to which these influences contribute to various dimensions of antisocial behavior and, subsequently, the extent to which interventions can alter liabilities and improve outcomes. Future attempts to identify underlying generators of antisocial behavior must employ sophisticated modern designs and technologies that enable researchers to directly examine brain function and environmental triggers in relation to behavioral outcome. The following items propose ways in which integrated research can be advanced and improved:

1. Great precision is necessary to identify subjects who meet criteria for *chronic* antisocial behaviors, selecting for early childhood conduct disorders, persistent aggressiveness, ADHD, negative affect, and early onset of drug use. Single, isolated behaviors are generally a product of a situation, rather than a pattern or orientation that may have biological origins. There is an obvious need for further longitudinal studies for wider availability of such subjects. Once subjects have been accurately classified, we can estimate the degree to which neurobiological factors influence offending, relative to and in interaction with social contributions.

2. Real-world conditions can be re-created to some degree within a laboratory setting by introducing a challenge or provocation during collection of biological measures. Passive or "resting state" conditions do not generate the sorts of physiological and biochemical responses that are often associated with antisocial behavior. In the midst of a heated argument in a bar, antisocial behavior can be more easily triggered in a susceptible person than in a laboratory with a technician standing watch. It is unnecessary, however, that subjects behave outwardly during the session when accurate behavioral classifications are in place. Instead, provocative tasks, like a specially designed computer game that elicits stressful responses, are more likely to elicit deviant biological responses in subjects with impaired impulse control and other relevant features than control subjects. So even under conditions where the subject is able to suppress behavioral responses, less likely is their ability to suppress biological ones. One such study pairs brain imaging (PET or fMRI) with a task that challenges cognitive abilities to assess differences in the function of the prefrontal cortex between drug abusers and nonusers, or juvenile delinquents and controls (see the box on page 88 for an example).

3. To begin to tease out relative influences of genetics and the environment, a concerted effort must be made to more carefully examine social and environmental experiences of subjects than most studies do at present. For example, the collection of genetically informative groups, such as twins and adopted children, permits estimates of relative gene-environment contributions. Molecular genetic approaches, on the other hand, assess static variations in neurotransmitter function, with the potential to eventually identify precise brain mechanisms that characterize antisocial behavior. Used in combination with rigorous measures of socio-environmental influences, these contemporary techniques hold great promise for an integrated science. As mentioned previously, present studies considered to be "multidisciplinary" tend to *control for*, rather than directly assess, relative influences of socio-environmental factors. A conceptual framework must be created for the integration of social and biological variables to enhance comprehensiveness, predictive ability, and treatment implications, and to avoid the tendency to reduce human behavior down to solely its biological roots (biological reductionism).

4. To understand brain-environmental relationships, their underlying mechanisms, and ability to change them, the following questions must be answered: (1) How can we assess environmental-neurobiological influences and then design interventions that impact at critical points in an individual's development to alter risk status? (2) If the genetic complement and biological conditions set the stage for responses to information from the environment, can environmental interventions change the behavioral outcome? (3) Can the environment be altered to improve brain function? (4) Will the behavioral outcome of this impact be sufficiently measurable?

6–1   *Using Imaging Techniques with Provocation*

One way to identify differences in brain function between people with a behavioral problem and those without is to use an imaging technique during some sort of cognitive or behavioral challenge. At the National Institute on Drug Abuse, in their intramural Brain Imaging Center, researchers are using positron emission tomography, or PET, to image the function of the brain. Among other measures, PET provides an estimate of glucose metabolism in various portions of the brain while a person performs a task. Given the literature which suggests that drug abusers may have impairments in cognitive abilities, studies are being conducted that require the subject to perform a cognitive task while the PET scans the brain to assess the rate of glucose metabolism. So far, findings suggest that drug abusers have lower rates of metabolism in certain areas of the brain responsible for cognitive abilities that involve regulation of behavior and emotional responses. The implications of these findings are twofold: that people susceptible to drug abuse may have functional brain impairments that interfere with their ability to assess consequences of their actions and act on that assessment, and/or that prior drug use produces and/or exacerbates these impairments. Either way, it is critical that treatments for drug abusers address these deficits and attempt to strengthen cognitive abilities (see Figure 6–1).

One example of an integrated research design is the examination of changes in brain function in response to an intervention. The combination of brain imaging, neuropsychological, and behavioral measures before, during, and after an intervention can be used to demonstrate a trend toward normal brain function and behavior over time. Thus, the biological impact of a treatment can be assessed by combining assessment techniques to evaluate change in both brain function and related behaviors.

CONTROVERSIAL ISSUES

Critics of biobehavior research worry that, in looking for criminal predispositions, researchers rely on oversimplified views of genetic and biological influences and of criminal behavior. Critics also worry that even if this research is

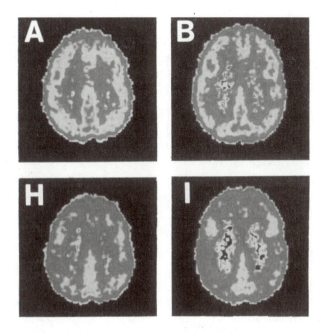

FIGURE **6-1**

Sometimes "your brain on drugs" is not like something in a frying pan, a popular analogy; it is more like something in the refrigerator. As these positron emission tomography (PET) scans show, the brain has lower metabolism and lower overall activity under the influence of cocaine than it has ordinarily. The darker areas indicate highest levels of activity, followed by yellow, green, and blue. A and B represent brain activity under normal conditions; H and I show activity after a cocaine injection.

focused entirely on individuals and is apolitical on its face, it will be publicly perceived as supporting racial stereotypes and justifying repressive social policies. At the same time, some of the opposition to the research arises from a concern that these studies may be used in efforts to establish racial differences in genetic predisposition or to justify conservative programs of social control.

The issues that arise in discussions of biological mechanisms in criminal behavior fall into two categories: philosophical and scientific problems; and social, moral, and ethical implications of the research findings.

Philosophical and Scientific Concerns

The philosophical and scientific issues that arise with this research involve, first, the potential that claims will be made for causal relationships between biology and crime. These problems raise questions about the ways in which the brain interacts with the physical and social environment. Which is a more powerful influence on our behavior—our biology or the environment? Does the social setting and our experiences change brain function and, subsequently, alter our perceptions of reality? Or does the brain determine how we respond to information from the environment and, perhaps, in turn alter the nature of information we receive from the environment? These questions all come to mind in debates regarding environment-biology interactions.

Second, there are fears about the prospects for explaining voluntary actions in terms of neurobiological processes. This is called biological reductionism—reducing human behavior to its basic biological components and drives that motivate us. To what extent do we have free will to choose our actions and determine our fate? Many who oppose this research fear that an understanding of brain function and genetic conditions may compromise our conception of what it is to be human, make decisions, and be responsible for our behaviors. Our criminal justice system and, in fact, all institutions within our society are based on notions of free will. We are rewarded for "good behaviors" and are punished for behaving badly, with a belief that the way we behave is "willed" and we must own up to it. Thus, determinism of any sort—environmental determinants or biological determinants—has been rejected in favor of voluntary actions.

Third, opponents of this research are concerned about the possibility of finding biological predispositions to behaviors that are, in essence, socially defined. For example, if a biological "cause" for violence is discovered, then would that invalidate all sorts of violent behavior? What about violence during war times or as a defense or as a function of an intolerable political situation? Violence is largely a socially constructed concept which changes in response to political shifts, social trends, and legal responses. If a biological condition was found to explain violence, that would assume that violence was a static, cross-culturally defined phenomenon. And it is not. This particular concern was discussed earlier in the shortcomings section regarding the need to use measurable behavioral phenotypes, rather than legal or social conceptions of a behavior.

Social, Moral, and Ethical Implications

The other set of issues concerns the social, moral, and ethical implications of research on biology and crime. Critics and proponents of this research set it against the backdrop of two very different legacies. On the one hand, humanity has a long, dark history of "discovering" sources of inferiority in certain individuals or groups, then using the "discovery" to justify gross inequalities and coercive social programs. On the other hand, it has been a sign of progress and enlightenment to recognize that undesirable traits and behaviors often arise from biological or psychiatric problems, rather than moral defects, and to offer humane treatments rather than to impose harsh punishments. A number of legal, ethical, and political obstacles to the acceptance and application

6–2 *The Eugenics Movement*

The Philosopher George Santayana said, "Those who cannot remember the past are condemned to repeat it." This adage is appropriate to our current rush into the "gene age," which some people believe have some parallels in the eugenics movement of the early decades of the twentieth century. Eugenics was, quite literally, an effort to breed better human beings—by encouraging the reproduction of people with "good" genes and discouraging those with "bad" genes. Eugenicists effectively lobbied for social legislation to keep racial and ethnical groups separate, to restrict immigration from southern and eastern Europe, and to sterilize people considered "genetically unfit." Elements of the American eugenics movement were models for the Nazis, whose radical adaptation of eugenics culminated in the Holocaust.

It is important to remind yourself that the vast majority of eugenics work has been completely discredited. In the final analysis, the eugenic description of human life reflected political and social prejudices, rather than scientific facts. Even supposedly "scientific" terms used by eugenicists were often pervaded with prejudice against racial, ethnic, and disabled groups. Some terms have no scientific meaning today. For example, "feeblemindedness" was used as a catch-all for a number of real and supposed mental disabilities, and was a common "diagnosis" used to make members of ethnic and racial minority groups appear inferior. However, the past should not be censored to protect those who would be otherwise offended or to hide from these human errors in judgment—to do so would distort the past and diminish the significance of the lessons to be learned from these events.

DNA Learning Center, Cold Spring Harbor Laboratory, *http://vector.cshl.org/eugenics/*

Readers who peruse this web site will see the product of a two-year review process conducted by the Eugenics Record Office at Cold Spring Harbor, which was the center of American eugenics research from 1910–1940. In the Archive, you will see numerous reports, articles, charts, and pedigrees that were considered scientific "facts" in their day.

Some groups and organizations fear that the identification of genes within the entire human genome may, once again, foster the desire of a few transgressors to cleanse the human race, by breeding a "superior"

(continued)

class of people and eliminating "dirty genes" that may contaminate our species. Thus, knowledge of these unspeakable past events is considered to be essential so that we avoid a repeat of the past. Proponents of this work, however, cite the very important medical advances we have made through the Human Genome Project and similar efforts toward a better understanding and more effective treatment of the various ills that plague us, for example, Alzheimer's Disease, Parkinson's Disease, Depression, and so on.

of biological and medical information by the CJS are covered extensively elsewhere (Fishbein & Thatcher, 1991; Jeffery, 1985; Marsh & Katz, 1985).

At the very least, care must be taken not to stigmatize or otherwise traumatize individuals or groups that are, as yet, innocent of a criminal or a civil violation. As researchers, we must avoid applying labels to behaviors we do not fully understand. Even in the event that biological measures are shown to be reliable and valid predictors of behavior and mental status, several serious civil rights and constitutional issues demand careful consideration. What if we were able to identify individuals very early in life who are at risk for antisocial behavior? Are we obligated to intervene—to provide an effective treatment? Do we mandate treatment? In cases in which a conviction is upheld, for example, forced compliance with a prevention or treatment regimen might result from findings that a biological abnormality played a role in an individual's antisocial behavior. Doing so in the absence of a proven violation of law would raise some eyebrows in most societies. The prediction of dangerousness is, in fact, a dangerous business! One must recognize the numerous legal and ethical concerns generated by such a strategy. To avoid these difficulties, a collaborative, multidisciplinary approach might be forged strictly to identify underlying sources of antisocial behaviors and minimize their occurrence in the population using both a public health and mental health approach (see Chapter 7). Prior to committing an offense, it is critical that the CJS does not become involved in detection or intervention efforts.

And the Debate Continues . . .

Advocates of this research hope that its findings will be used to prevent crime and violence by recognizing the warning signs and intervening before its onset, with benefits to both potential perpetrators and potential victims. Critics fear that the research will lead to large-scale neglect and abuse. Its actual or reported findings may convince legislators that social and economic reforms are doomed to failure because they attempt to apply social solutions to a biological problem. Critics also believe that viewing crime as a medical problem to

6–3 *Multiple-Personality Defense Goes to High Court HeraldNet.com 2/16/00*

EVERETT—A sex offender's multiple-personality defense, barred by a trial judge and the state Supreme Court, is being taken before the U.S. Supreme Court with support from his victim, a woman who was his therapist in prison. "You don't see that very often," said lawyer David Koch of Seattle, who is handling William Greene's appeal.

The victim, attacked by Greene after his release from imprisonment on a 1988 indecent-liberties conviction, wanted to testify for the defense in 1995, when Greene went to trial in Snohomish County Superior Court on indecent-liberties charges in the attack on her. But the trial judge barred testimony about the multiple-personalities disorder she had diagnosed. Greene's conviction, his "third strike," sent him to the state penitentiary at Walla Walla for life.

In September, the state Supreme Court upheld the trial judge's decision, all but ruling out use of a multiple-personality defense in criminal cases on grounds that expert testimony cannot help jurors decide responsibility. The justices referred to a state evidence rule that requires scientific testimony be "helpful" to jurors. Koch, who contends Greene's rights were violated by the decision, plans to file a petition with the nation's highest court this week. He contends the state justices went too far.

Prosecutors disagree. "I read the opinion as basically saying the state of scientific knowledge doesn't tell us anything about responsibility, which is what we care about in criminal trials," said Seth Fine, chief criminal appellate lawyer for Snohomish County.

In therapeutic settings, a person with multiple personalities is referred to as "the system," Fine said. The system is held accountable for misdeeds. The therapist began treating Greene at the Twin Rivers correctional facility in Monroe. Greene grew up in California reformatories after being declared incorrigible at age 8.

The therapist, 50, of Snohomish County, said she diagnosed more than 20 personalities in Greene, now 45. Snohomish County prosecutors believe Greene, also diagnosed as an antisocial personality who uses guile, charm or force to get his way, is faking. Before trial, prosecutors argued the disorder was too controversial among psychiatric experts to be admitted as scientific evidence. The judge agreed.

(continued)

Koch appealed Greene's conviction to the state Court of Appeals, which in August 1998 ordered a new trial, saying multiple-personality disorder meets the standard for scientific evidence. The state Supreme Court disagreed last fall, ruling that no new trial was needed.

As you can readily see from this story, the legal system is unprepared for testimony that includes a defense based on psychiatric state. This is also true for evidence based on biological defect or disturbance, which is often present in psychiatric disorders. Not only are we often unable to always discriminate between an actual diagnosis and a fabricated one, the science to establish a cause (disorder) and effect (crime) is not yet well developed.

be treated, rather than as a response to oppressive social and economic conditions or as a matter of individual choice, may result in policies that are patronizing, disrespectful, and highly coercive. On the other hand, advocates argue that if we continue to examine only 50 percent of the equation (the social causes), then we will continue to mistreat the problem and support programs with very low success rates.

Critics argue vehemently that biological research must be seen in the context of our racial history and racist attitudes. In our society, any research that links criminal behavior to biological features may be mistakenly seen as implicating the African American community and contribute to its stigmatization. Many Americans see violent crime as a minority problem, in part because of the disproportionate number of African Americans in prison, and in part because of deep prejudices that make violent crime seem more characteristic of Blacks than Whites. Defenders of the research, however, deny that it must be captive to our racial history, and argue that it will ultimately do far more to *alleviate* than exacerbate racial tensions. Because this research focuses on both biological deviations and adverse social circumstances that trigger the expression of existing vulnerabilities, it may highlight the profound impact that adverse environmental factors can have. More specifically, over two hundred years of racial discrimination has resulted in the relegation of a large proportion of our African American citizens to impoverished and underserved communities. No where do we see a greater concentration of "environmental triggers" and adversity in these neighborhoods, which contributes in substantial ways to maladaptive behaviors, irrespective of genetic or biological traits. Thus, we may eventually be able to concentrate on and alleviate those social problems that are differentially and disproportionately distributed throughout our society and which trigger underlying vulnerabilities and lead to an increased prevalence of various behavioral disorders (see David Wasserman's [University of Maryland] discussion from the Genetics and Crime conference in Maryland, 1995).

SUMMARY

This chapter highlighted many of the shortcomings in design, measurement, and interpretation often cited in biobehavioral research. It should be emphasized, once again, that while some of these deficiencies are more common in the biological sciences, others characterize many forms of human behavioral research, including techniques used in the social sciences. No study or body of research is without criticism. This reasoning does not excuse us from acknowledging these deficiencies or attempting to rectify them. Instead, it reveals that in spite of the tremendous strides we have taken lately to understand human behavior, there is still much left unanswered and equivocal. It is clear, even so, that when we are able to break down disciplinary boundaries and work together in teams that represent many perspectives and technical skills, the answers will become more accessible.

No matter how this research is viewed, there is ample reason to use caution against the premature application of findings from the biobehavioral findings within the CJS. The weaknesses in design, sampling techniques, and statistical procedures described earlier prevent us from drawing definitive conclusions from some studies. And for certain areas of research, the results are not consistent. Policies and programs based on solid and reproducible findings save time and money and potentially protect individual rights and community safety.

PRACTICAL AND POLICY IMPLICATIONS

There is a growing awareness that if we begin to increase multidisciplinary research on chronic criminality, early onset of delinquency, violence, and involvement of drug abuse in crime, the strength and effectiveness of criminal justice (CJ) interventions will be substantially enhanced. To form a scientific and empirical foundation for emerging CJ policies and practices, it is critical that researchers begin to incorporate findings from various subdisciplines within the behavioral sciences. Because CJ practitioners and scholars are instrumental in the design and implementation of criminal justice practices and policies, their involvement, familiarity, and scrutiny are critical to the field's development. Teams of researchers from relevant disciplines and practitioners from both correctional and clinical settings can engage in a unique and powerful exchange between theory, empirical research, and practice.

The present Director of the National Institute on Drug Abuse, Dr. Alan Leschner, maintains that "science must replace ideology" before drug abuse can be fully understood, treated, and prevented. In other words, our beliefs about why certain behaviors occur and the rationale for the techniques we use should be backed by scientific evidence. The same is true for the study of all antisocial behaviors. Science must inform ideology as a basis for inquiries within the CJS and for the development of effective treatment, prevention, and policy strategies. A focus on individual differences, their origins, modulators, and interactions with social variables, is crucial. We need to be more creative, innovative, and scientific than approaches used in the past. The fields of criminology and criminal justice are devoted to the study of human behavior and the "control" of antisocial behaviors which harm others. Findings within the behavioral sciences suggest that "control" is best achieved through effective means of preventing and treating those characteristics that underlie antisocial behaviors. Thus, an understanding of underlying mechanisms will lead to more effective, research-based targeted interventions.

One of the most pressing issues within corrections today, for example, is the presence of violent inmates who do not respond to existing treatments, are unresponsive to authority, repeatedly violate institutional rules, victimize within the institution, and are responsible for high post-release recidivism rates. Research suggests that a substantial proportion of these inmates have psychopathic characteristics which further complicate treatment efforts and worsen their post-release outcomes. At present, there are very few attempts to treat these inmates, and most efforts have failed. In the absence of a thorough understanding of what underlies their persistent violence and treatment resistance, the system will continue to fail to reach this very important subgroup which is known to commit the majority of serious, violent crimes.

Evidence is mounting from multidisciplinary research and clinical investigations to suggest that impairments in executive cognitive function (impulsivity and poor decision-making ability) are prevalent in this recidivistic subgroup. As described earlier, these sorts of impairments are thought to play a significant role in violence and psychopathy, and potentially explain the seemingly callous disregard for threats of punishment, rules and values, and future consequences, as well as an excessive need for stimulation and reward. Because ECF (executive cognitive function) impairments are alterable, they often respond favorably to targeted treatment approaches. Incorporating this knowledge into criminal justice policies and practices could alter their course substantially to dramatically improve ability to assess, detect, and treat offenders who are, otherwise, considered intractable.

PREREQUISITES FOR PRACTICAL APPLICATION

Before we can begin to design and implement programs and policies based on this science which may have an impact on criminal offending, the relevance and significance of biological perspectives for criminology must be fully evaluated. The following prerequisites must be met:

1. Estimate the incidence of biological disorders among antisocial populations.
2. Identify etiologic or causal mechanisms.
3. Assess the dynamic interaction among biological and socio-environmental factors.
4. Determine whether improvements in behavior follow large-scale therapeutic manipulations.

Each task is described in more detail here.

Estimating the Incidence of Biological Disorders in Offenders

At this first stage of scientific inquiry into ways in which the biobehavioral sciences can be applied to criminology, researchers are charged with determining the incidence of the many possible disorders with biological involvement that are present among offenders. We have found compelling evidence to suggest that both biological and social disadvantages are more prevalent in this population than in the general population. Certain mental illnesses and personality disorders, which have been associated with particular biological traits, are more common. For example, there is a large body of research to suggest that individuals who exhibit violent, impulsive, and disregulated behavior have lower levels of serotonin activity, on average, among other irregular features, than those who do not exhibit such behavior. And also, serotonin is very sensitive to stressful environmental experiences. There are numerous such interactions between biological and environmental factors that influence antisocial behaviors. Nevertheless, the extent of biological involvement remains unknown; behavioral disorders can result from many diverse influences. Once prevalence rates are known for biologically and genetically influenced forms of behavioral disorders in relevant populations, we can better determine how substantially an intervention strategy that incorporates biological and genetic findings may influence the problems associated with antisocial conduct. At a minimum, however, indications are that a significant number of criminal offenders and troubled youth may suffer from some type of underlying pathology which suggests the need for early identification and intervention.

Determining Causality

The second task is to identify the causal mechanisms involving genetic and biological factors that influence an individual's risk status in combination with environmental conditions. So far, correlations are significant for relationships between antisocial behavior and particular personality, neurochemical, and physiological traits that have a genetic base in many studies (see, e.g., Fishbein, 1990; Mednick et al., 1987; Raine, 1993; Reiss et al., 1994). Similarly, twin, adoption, and molecular genetic studies are suggesting that genetic effects on antisocial behavior including aggressiveness and substance abuse may be important (Cadoret et al., 1986; Carey, 1992; Cloninger et al., 1982; Mednick et al., 1987; Rowe, 1986). These studies are not, however, able to identify mechanisms by which "high risk" traits may be inherited or to demonstrate precisely which biological systems are being affected by genetic factors. The "markers" or correlates for antisocial behavior involve biological functions that may or may not be due to the expression of genes; they are also strongly influenced by environmental conditions. Recent work in neurobiology and molecular genetics will likely generate a more rigorous understanding of the mechanisms involved.

Proceedings within the criminal justice system require a more reliable identification of causal relationships than we are now able to provide using any known set of standards. Bail, release on recognizance, determination of competency, determination of guilt, sentencing options, probation, and parole decisions all pertain to the ability to establish the (1) commission of a crime, (2) mental state or mens rea indicative of intent, and (3) proclivity to recidivate. There are stringent guidelines that must be followed for various types of evidence that speak to these conditions to be admitted into courtroom proceedings, particularly with regard to biological and genetic measures which are unfamiliar to the criminal justice profession. Similar to other forms of evidence, the state of biological and genetic research must be thoroughly scientifically tested, reliable, and agreed upon by everyone in the courtroom in order to meet criteria to establish causality. The inclusion of both social and biological variables in research and eventually in individual assessments will enhance the ability to make these determinations given the substantially increased potential to know both sides of the equation—nature plus nurture—rather than only half.

Assessing the Interaction between Biology and the Environment

To further establish the relevance of and applications for biology to criminology, we must demonstrate the ability to reliably predict antisocial behavior using a combination of biological and social variables. The central question thus becomes: Can we explain more of the variance in the incidence of antisocial behavior with an integrated approach than with an unidisciplinary (single field) perspective? Many clinicians and researchers have concluded that predicting antisocial behavior with social or legal variables is inherently unreliable (Cozzoza & Steadman, 1974; Gottfredson, 1986; Monahan, 1981; Wenk et al., 1972). Prediction studies incorporating biological measures into sociological databases promise to significantly increase the predictive and explanatory power of conditions associated with antisocial behavior.

The inclusion of biological measures holds promise in explaining individual variation within a social context. Why is it, for example, that not all children exposed to child abuse become violent as adults? Research suggests that whether child abuse contributes to violent behavior partially depends on the presence of a biological vulnerability, for example, brain damage, low serotonin, or an underactive ANS. Perhaps abused children without existing or resulting brain damage would be less aggressive and more in control of their impulses. Research yet to be conducted may also show that individuals with biological "disadvantages" respond with more violent or criminal behavior in a criminogenic environment than those equipped with biological "insulators" or protective factors, for example, high intelligence or adequate serotonin activity.

Brizer and Crowner (1989) aptly note that the actual study of our ability to predict dangerousness suffers from methodological limitations and, as a result, we cannot conclude that valid prediction is impossible. Studies reviewed in their text indicate that if we include biological variables (e.g., integrity of central nervous system function) we may, indeed, enhance predictive ability if dispositional (temperament and other features considered "innate") and situational factors are considered as interacting forces. In a separate study illustrative of this approach, Virkkunen et al. (1989) examined a selected set of behavioral and psychobiological variables to identify predictors of recidivism in a sample of violent offenders and arsonists. Their results suggested that recidivism is best predicted using a combination of behavioral and psychobiological variables, rather than with behavioral variables alone. Numerous studies in more recent years provide credence to these findings, reporting, for example, that prenatal conditions in combination with poor parenting predict behavioral problems in the offspring, or that the combination of prefrontal dysfunction in the brain and social adversity predicts delinquency.

An integrated study of the effects of numerous environmental and biological variables on criminal behavior, juvenile delinquency, and disciplinary problems was conducted by Denno. Denno (1990) concluded that "biological and environmental variables exert strong and independent influences on juvenile crime" and that "crime appears to be directly related to familial instability and, most important, a lack of behavioral control associated with neurological and central nervous system disorders." She cautioned, however, that behavior should be predicted in terms of a series of probabilities of expected behavior, not in terms of cause and effect. Future research into practical problems in criminology may find considerable solutions in an approach that neither neglects nor places undue emphasis on socio-environmental or biological features of behavior.

Assessing Effects of Therapeutic Manipulations

The final stage of scientific inquiry requires that researchers be able to manipulate and control antisocial behavior, in this context with biological variables. Reliable behavioral changes attributable to biological treatments have yet to be demonstrated in offenders; however, such manipulations in clinical settings have produced some remarkable results, particularly in those prone to violence. One particularly visible example of the application of biological data is the treatment of sex offenders using medications, a practice called pharmacotherapy. Antiandrogen agents (e.g., Depo-Provera), which compete with male hormones believed to be partially responsible for sexual deviance, are administered in some clinics to suppress sex drive and, consequently, sex offending. Some research indicates that this approach has been moderately successful (Berlin, 1983; Berlin & Meinecke, 1981; Bradford, 1983; Cordoba & Chapel, 1983; Murray, 1987; Spodak et al., 1978). These findings are in stark contrast to more conventional methods of treating sex offenders, which are primarily counseling-based, that have quite high failure rates. Others, however, criticize the approach because of (1) the equivocal findings that provide empirical support, (2) the fact that the behaviors sometimes resurface when the drug is discontinued, (3) its experimental nature, (4) the issue of forced compliance, and (5) evidence that only nonviolent sex offenders respond to antiandrogen treatment (see Demsky, 1984). Another example is the use of medications to control violent behavior, particularly Intermittent Explosive Disorders (Coccaro et al., 1999). Anticonvulsants and certain antidepressants have been found highly effective in many cases (Fava, 1999). Importantly, these drugs do not tranquilize or alter personality. Instead, they enable the patient to self-regulate their behavior and they reduce irritability. In either event, biological management techniques require further scientific support and, even more important, time for the legal system to become acquainted with their premises in order to establish appropriate guidelines.

It is perhaps unreasonable to expect a complete behavioral overhaul following a biological treatment, even when a disorder has been properly identified. One of the central tenets of this text is that behavior is a result of a dynamic interaction among many diverse social and biological conditions. The appropriate administration of a medication or other treatment may certainly be warranted for some individuals with identifiable pathology. However, this approach used alone undermines the proposal that multiple factors are responsible for behavior. Manipulating *only* biological variables will not necessarily produce complete behavioral change—other interacting contributions must be attended to also. Once an individual has entered the criminal justice system, behavioral problems are substantially compounded and the treatment of only one condition does not yield adequate therapeutic results. Thus, it is critical that in addition to medication when indicated, the individual should also receive supportive counseling, behavior modification strategies, and a change in aspects of the environment that are contributing to the behavioral difficulties.

ENHANCING THE RIGOR OF ASSESSMENTS AND TREATMENTS

One overriding practical goal of this research is to develop assessment tools that can be readily used within both correctional and clinical settings to identify individuals at high risk for violence, psychopathic behavior, drug abuse, and other types of persistent antisocial behaviors. Studies suggest that certain biological vulnerabilities, in interaction with adverse social conditions, may underlie these behaviors and are more prevalent within offender populations. Using multivariate (measuring several variables at once) assessment instruments, offenders can be triaged or subtyped on the basis of underlying disorders for targeted treatments. Because offenders who do not respond to conventional treatments often possess underlying susceptibilities and adverse social conditions that compound their problems, and are particularly at risk for persistent serious criminality and substance abuse, this subgroup requires more intensive and customized approaches. Accordingly, offenders will be better equipped to maintain control over their own behavior rather than requiring severe methods of external restraint that are terminated when they are released.

Treatment efforts that focus on the underlying mechanisms in antisocial behaviors will more likely succeed in reversing or redirecting these behavioral outcomes. Successful regimens attempt to comprehensively identify the unique underlying mechanisms in an individual's antisocial behavior and may employ a combination of pharmaceutical, behavioral, cognitive, and family therapies. Nevertheless, while a clinical approach to treatment and prevention may be achieved with knowledge of individual risks and vulnerabilities, global prevention and intervention programs can be implemented now to increase resiliency to prevailing risk factors in a population. Building safety nets, providing resources for those without opportunities, increasing availability of alternative modes of behavior, revitalizing neighborhoods, assembling multidisciplinary teams to intervene, and enhancing community involvement could have an immediate impact on the problem by providing some protection for those who are particularly "vulnerable."

For example, recognition that a deprived environment can induce below normal levels of nervous system arousal, or that stress lowers serotonin activity, may enhance our understanding of why some individuals under these circumstances develop an unusual need for stimulation, often expressed as risk-taking behaviors, particularly when there are no other constructive alternatives available to them. Manipulations of the social environment, therefore, may profoundly alter an individual's biological stamina, possibly improving impulse control and coping mechanisms.

IMPLICATIONS FOR PREVENTION STRATEGIES

We are also closer to enacting prevention programs aimed at entire communities, neighborhoods, or schools which are at risk for exposure to biological and socio-environmental hazards that are known to increase the incidence of behavioral problems. Factors that may prove to be important contributors to relevant behavioral disorders could then be manipulated on a wide scale to prevent the onset of behavioral disorders in the general population. Early detection programs could be implemented by school systems, and parents could be educated to recognize signs of an impairment. Screening clinics, regulating environmental toxins, school programs, prenatal care facilities, and public educational programs are only a few of the preventative measures possible. The number of "risk" factors could, in essence, be reduced or minimized.

An excellent example of this strategy was suggested by Moffitt and her colleagues in their review of minor physical anomalies (MPAs), that is, observable minor malformations that result from a disturbance in fetal development. MPAs are reflective of other hidden abnormalities, such as CNS impairment, that may result from some perinatal trauma (e.g., illness, poor diet, drug use, or stress). A relatively large number of MPAs have been observed among hyperactive and violent populations. There is no acceptable mode of individual remediation in such cases, particularly because of the remote association of MPAs with behavior. These consistent observations, however, emphasize the need for a global effort to provide proper prenatal care. Such programs may reduce the incidence of developmental deficits related to behavioral disorders.

THE POTENTIAL IMPACT ON CRIMINAL JUSTICE POLICIES

This mixture of scientific and pragmatic approaches to studying and managing antisocial behavior promises to further improve our potential to improve CJ policies. Informing the criminal justice, mental health, and public health systems of this genre of research findings is critical to addressing the triggers (both causal and exacerbating) in the social environment that can contribute to antisocial behaviors in susceptible individuals. Incorporating this knowledge regarding underlying generators of antisocial behavior into CJ policies will reach a greater proportion of the population than will individual treatment programs, and will contribute eventually to large-scale systemwide policy changes, such as in bail, pretrial detention, sentencing and release decisions, as well as child rearing and school practices. The availability of more effective treatments for various antisocial behaviors will most likely compel the general public and policy-makers to consider alternative official responses to criminal conduct. An understanding of underlying mechanisms in violence has the potential to produce more favorable treatment outcomes in offenders and to develop more humane policies that will have preventative effects.

PROSPECTIVE APPLICATIONS

Clinical approaches, based on the medical or mental health models, hold the most promise for the eventual application of treatments that result from biological and genetic research, with an understanding that they must, for the most part, be individualized and consented to by the "patient." Unfortunately, however, only those who are economically and opportunistically privileged in our society have access to clinical settings. Those who are less privileged are denied access due to a variety of systemwide conditions and are often relegated to the criminal justice system instead. Although the criminal justice system has a notorious reputation for doling out tranquilizers and mood stabilizers, these medications have custodial (i.e., maintenance and security), not therapeutic, purposes. Cases with biomedical involvement, sometimes genetically influenced, could instead be managed by the mental health system, possibly within secure facilities for those deemed dangerous.

This approach is particularly appropriate for use in drug abuse and addiction. A majority of offenders in our correctional facilities are nonviolent, drug users. In other words, while serious and violent offenders threaten society, create disorder, and victimize individuals, *most* substance abusers and addicts threaten only themselves. Rather than incarceration, costing billions of dollars and usurping precious space, drug addicts could receive appropriate treatment, sensitive to the needs of the individual, with strong benefits to the offender, the family, and the greater society. And given that drug addicts are more likely to engage in criminal activity, it is reassuring to know that crime decreases dramatically in drug addicts in treatment. Recovery can be achieved if effective treatment is available. Still, 75 percent of our federal and state funds for drug abuse are provided to law enforcement, an approach recognized by experts to be an inadequate remedy.

Clinicians may eventually be able to identify individuals at risk if they are armed with the knowledge of social, biological, and genetic traits that increase risk. When this information becomes available, more effective interventions, earlier in developmental stages, can be provided. Children will be better equipped to overcome disadvantages, social or genetic, and reach their potential. Adults will be better equipped to maintain control over their own behavior, rather than requiring external restraints, such as jail or mental institutions. Research consistently indicates that far fewer crimes are committed when individuals are actively in treatment than when they do not receive treatment (see Fishbein, 1991; Fishbein & Pease, 1996). For drug users in particular, the length of treatment is negatively related to crime and drug use. If treatments or alternatives remain unavailable and ineffective, individuals at risk will likely continue to fall through the cracks and engage in crime and drug abuse.

Before we are ready to apply a clinical approach that focuses on biological and genetic vulnerabilities in antisocial behavior, legal professionals should be charged with the responsibility of scrutinizing the research, and creating statutes to guide its application. The likelihood of abuse is greater if such research is not made public and regulated. Consent and compliance are also pertinent issues, and related questions must be answered by legal scholars and ethicists before research influences policy. Can we enforce compliance with treatment? Will coercive treatments be effective? Many argue that treatment is much more humane than techniques we currently resort to, including incarceration, solitary confinement, capital punishment, or even neglect for underlying precursors. We do not presently require consent for punishment or even execution. To what extent do we require consent for treatment? These questions must be addressed before we proceed.

The Public Health Approach

In contrast to the medical approach is the public health model which orchestrates global primary prevention programs aimed at populations at risk. Based on the notion that interpersonal violence is a public health problem (Rosenberg & Mercy, 1986), widescale manipulations may be implemented to prevent the development of a problem and lessen the toll in illness, death, and quality of life without stigmatization. "The key to prevention may lie in greater understanding of the behavioral components that contribute to violence" (Spivak et al., 1988:1341). For example, convincing evidence was described earlier that later behavioral problems are associated with perinatal complications (Denno, 1990; Mednick & Kandel, 1988; Raine et al., 1994). An appropriate public health approach would be to provide readily available prenatal care, particularly to populations without ready access to medical care. A public health approach strives to insulate vulnerable individuals from the effects of a criminogenic, high-risk environment, increasing resiliency by building safety nets and resources in a community. Such strategies are proposed to work regardless of the origins of behavior.

Contrary to popular belief, biological and genetic traits are not static and unchangeable; they can be altered in a social environment conducive to change. Thus, theoretically, large-scale social programs can lead to behavioral improvements even in cases where the propensities are genetically influenced by minimizing the impact of an environment that would otherwise be conducive to antisocial behavior.

Educational, social, economic, and behavioral programs all minimize the impact of an environment and a biological constitution conducive to antisocial behavior. Adverse interactions in the home such as physical abuse, parental absenteeism, and poor discipline practices exacerbate the child's innate liability to behavioral disorders. Also, association with peers promoting antisocial behavior is related to the combined influence of an innate negative affect and deficient parental monitoring. These findings indicate how, among high-risk individuals, adverse interactions with the social environment can orient the child toward enhanced risk for a negative outcome. The quality of interaction between the person having a particular biological disposition, and the social environment which determines the behavior response patterns and emotional reactions should be the focus in interventions. Universal programs that target these risk factors to minimize their impact particularly on vulnerable, high-risk individuals include:

- Proper prenatal care
- Postnatal home visitation
- Rehabilitation for pregnant drug abusers
- Educational campaigns and enrichment programs
- Teacher training and parenting education

- Antibullying programs
- School-based conflict resolution and skill building
- After-school programs
- Reduction of television and other media violence
- Gun control
- Identification and treatment of learning disabilities
- Drug and alcohol treatment

While the potential benefits are apparent, the public health approach also raises civil liberties issues pertaining to rights to privacy, freedom from unwanted disclosures, and ethical considerations concerning widescale medical and social surveillance of select populations (Rosenfeld & Decker, 1993). Such interventions may extend services to those who do not want them, have potential to further victimize underprivileged classes, and may compromise personal freedoms (Hawkins, 1989; Kittrie, 1971; Marx, 1985). Adverse consequences must be minimized by providing necessary safeguards for personal rights and liberties. On the other hand, however, "what rights and liberties [do the] beneficiaries of violence prevention programs currently enjoy [?]." Many of those ". . . who would be directly affected by the interventions cannot safely walk the streets and have already had many basic legal rights curtailed because they are under control of the criminal justice system. The issue . . . then, may not be whether their freedom will be endangered by violence prevention programs, but how such programs might improve their lives while they are under custody and reduce their risk for violence after they are released" (Rosenfeld & Decker, 1993:31–32).

SPECIAL ISSUES FOR THE CRIMINAL JUSTICE SYSTEM

Unlike other disciplines, results of research on offenders can have direct implications for the management and control of antisocial individuals and those at high risk for offending. There are concerns in the field that findings of biological studies could lead to inappropriate or involuntary medical treatment in the criminal justice system and the possibility that individuals who are at high risk, but have not yet engaged in criminal behavior, may be prematurely targeted for these control measures. Hypocritically, however, tactics of the present criminal justice system that routinely incarcerates (with racial prejudice) the mentally ill and drug addicts who are desperately in need of treatment, not incarceration, have not been effectively challenged. Moreover, rather than intervening in cases where children's rights are visibly being violated (e.g., abuse or neglect) or special needs remain unattended (learning disabilities)—conditions known to increase risk for delinquency—society customarily waits until their problems are compounded and they are old enough to incarcerate.

Treatment of individuals with similar behavior problems in a clinical setting demonstrates that effective methods are available in many cases (see Fishbein, 1999). It is considered medical malpractice to withhold effective treatment in the medical field, which is a dictate in marked contrast to practices of the criminal justice system. Treatments of many varieties, when appropriately dispensed, increase individual self-control rather than require the external restraints of the criminal justice system.

Criminal justice policies must be based on well-founded theories and findings that survive scientific scrutiny. The application of scientific findings to criminal justice programs that are well recognized and accepted by the discipline have more value than trial and error approaches in preventing or minimizing antisocial behavior. Although biological techniques in the assessment of human behavior are still under the microscope and definitive answers have yet to surface, the foregoing description of biological foundations for behavior provides evidence of their applicability and value. By undertaking a collaborative strategy, we can develop more effective prevention and therapeutic programs, and develop a legal system that reflects public consensus, meets human needs, and maintains an ethical and organized social structure.

E. O. Wilson, a leading figure in evolutionary approaches to the study of behavior, and one of the most distinguished scientific thinkers of our time, argues persuasively in favor of integration between the physical and social sciences by linking them with a single overarching theory (see Wilson, 1998). As disciplines converge, he argues, we will develop the ability to solve many of the world's most dire problems. "Most of the issues that vex humanity daily—ethnic conflict, arms escalation, overpopulation, abortion, environment, endemic poverty, to cite several most persistently before us—cannot be solved without integrating knowledge from the natural sciences with that of the social sciences and humanities." Not coincidentally (nor inclusively), many of these problems contribute in substantial ways to antisocial behavior, from violent criminal offending to white collar crime. Bridging the sciences will yield answers to questions that have alluded the field of criminology for decades. As a result, practices and programs that incorporate findings linking environmental stressors to biological impacts and vice versa are likely to produce improvements in integrity of social, psychosocial, and biological mechanisms. And more importantly, perhaps conclusions drawn from interdisciplinary research will promote the creation of socio-environmental conditions that are more sensitive to basic human needs and, accordingly, conducive to prosocial behavior.

SUMMARY AND CONCLUSIONS

Biological and genetic research highlights the important role of the environment in modulating both social and genetic instigators and can inform us of the value of primary prevention and public health strategies to curb antisocial behavior and violence. Interventions that are primarily social and educational can be employed to enhance environmental and biological insulators, as suggested above. It is not necessary to wait for biological and genetic research to demonstrate definite causal influences. We have known for decades which social forces are protective against both social and genetic risks and have neglected to adequately fund programs that will provide insulation.

Conducting biological and genetic research does not excuse us from supporting social programs, particularly given the ability of social approaches to positively affect behavior no matter what the origins. Nevertheless, interdisciplinary research is crucial if we are ever to provide needed services and treatments for individuals with compelling biological and genetic disadvantages. Studies suggest that a subgroup of our population suffers from biological and genetic vulnerabilities that overwhelm the influence of any environment. Not only do these individuals stand to greatly benefit from the research, but the public may eventually give way to more tolerance of behavioral aberrations, understanding that behavior is not entirely volitional at all times in all individuals. Instead of waiting until a vulnerable child becomes old enough to incarcerate perhaps early assistance will enable us to avoid the personal and financial expense of criminal justice system involvement. There is little evidence that present tactics are effective; thus, we need to move forward into an era of early intervention and compassionate treatment that biobehavioral research may advance.

References

Agid, O., B. Shapira, J. Zislin, M. Ritsner, B. Hanin, H. Murad, T. Troudart, M. Bloch, U. Heresco-Levy, and B. Lerer. 1999. Environment and vulnerability to major psychiatric illness: A case control study of early parental loss in major depression, bipolar disorder and schizophrenia [see comments]. *Molecular Psychiatry,* 4(2):163–72.

Albanese, A., G. Hamill, J. Jones, D. Skuse, D. R. Matthews, and R. Stanhope. 1994. Reversibility of physiological growth hormone secretion in children with psychosocial dwarfism. *Clinical Endocrinology* (Oxf), 40:687–92.

Allan, A. M., H. Wu, L. L. Paxton, and D. D. Savage. 1998. Prenatal ethanol exposure alters the modulation of the gamma-aminobutyric acidA1 receptor-gated chloride ion channel in adult rat offspring. *Journal of Pharmacology and Experimental Therapeutics,* 284:250–57.

Anisman, H., and R. M. Zacharko. 1986. Behavioral and neurochemical consequences associated with stressors. *Annals of the New York Academy of Sciences,* 467:205–25.

Archer, J. 1991. The influence of testosterone on human aggression. *British Journal of Psychology,* 82 (Pt 1):1–28.

Azuma, S. D., and I. J. Chasnoff. 1993. Outcome of children prenatally exposed to cocaine and other drugs: A path analysis of three-year data. *Pediatrics,* 92:396–402.

Backon, J. 1989. Etiology of alcoholism: Relevance of prenatal hormonal influences on the brain, anomalous dominance, and neurochemical and pharmacological brain asymmetry. *Medical Hypotheses,* 29:59–63.

Ballenger, J. C., F. K. Goodwin, L. F. Major, and G. L. Brown. 1979. Alcohol and central serotonin metabolism in man. *Archives of General Psychiatry,* 36:224–27.

Banks, T., and J. M. Dabbs. 1996. Salivary testosterone and cortisol in a delinquent and violent urban subculture. *Journal of Social Psychology,* 136:49–56.

Bardo, M. T., R. L. Donohew, and N. G. Harrington. 1996. Psychobiology of novelty seeking and drug seeking behavior. *Behavior and Brain Research,* May, 77(1–2):23–43. Review.

Barrat, E. S., A. Felthouse, T. Kent, M. J. Leibman, & D. D. Coates. 2000. Criterion measures of aggression-impulsive versus premeditated aggression. In D. Fishbein (Ed.) The Science Treatment and Prevention of Antisocial Behavior. New Jersey: Civic Research Institute, Inc.

Barratt, E. S., and J. H. Patton. 1983. Impulsivity: Cognitive, behavioral and psychophysiological correlates. In M. Zuckerman (ed.), *Biological bases of sensation seeking, impulsivity and anxiety* (pp. 77–116). Hillsdale, NJ: Erlbaum.

Barratt, E. S., and L. Slaughter. 1998. Defining, measuring, and predicting impulsive aggression: A heuristic model. *Behavioral Sciences and the Law.* 16(3):285–302.

Battaglia, G., T. M. Cabrera, and L. D. Van de Kar. 1994. Prenatal cocaine produces biochemical and functional changes in brain serotonin systems in rat progeny. *NIDA Research Monograph,* 158:115–48.

Beckham, J. C., M. E. Feldman, A. C. Kirby, M. A. Hertzberg, and S. D. Moore. 1997. Interpersonal violence and its correlates in Vietnam veterans with chronic posttraumatic stress disorder. *Journal of Clinical Psychology,* 53(8):859–69.

Begleiter, H., B. Porjesz, R. Rawlings, and M. Eckardt. 1987. Auditory recovery function and P3 in boys at high risk for alcoholism. *Alcohol,* 4:315–21.

Bell, R. Q., and M. F. Waldrop. 1992. Temperament and minor physical anomalies. Ciba Foundation Symposium, 89:206–20.

Belsky, J. 1980. Child maltreatment: An ecological integration. *American Psychologist,* 35:320–35.

———. 1993. Etiology of child maltreatment: A developmental-ecological analysis. *Psychological Bulletin,* 114:413–34.

———. 1997. Attachment, mating, and parenting. *Human Nature,* 8:361–81.

Belsky, J., S. Laurence, and P. Draper. 1991. Childhood experience, interpersonal development, and reproductive strategy: An evolutionary theory of socialization. *Child Development,* 62:647–70.

Benes, F. M. 1997. The role of stress and dopamine-GABA interactions in the vulnerability for schizophrenia. *Journal of Psychiatric Research,* 31:257–75.

Berenbaum, S. A., and S. M. Resnick. 1997. Early androgen effects on aggression in children and adults with congenital adrenal hyperplasia. *Psychoneuroendocrinology,* 22:505–15.

Bergman, B., and B. Brismar. 1994. Hormone levels and personality traits in abusive and suicidal male alcoholics. *Alcoholism Clinical and Experimental Research,* 18(2):311–16.

Berlin, F.S. 1983. Sex offenders: A biomedical perspective and a status report on biomedical treatment. In J. G. Greer and I. R. Stuart (eds.), *The sexual aggressor: Current perspectives on treatment.* New York: Van Nostrand Reinhold.

Berlin, F. S., and C. F. Meinecke. 1981. Treatment of sex offenders with antiandrogenic medication: Conceptualization, review of treatment modalities, and preliminary findings. *American Journal of Psychiatry,* 138:601–7.

Bioulac, B., M. Benezech, B. Renaud, B. Noel, and D. Roche. 1980. Serotoninergic dysfunction in the 47,XYY syndrome. *Biological Psychiatry,* 15:917–23.

Bjorklund D. F., and R. D. Brown. 1998. Physical play and cognitive development: Integrating activity, cognition, and education. *Child Development,* 69(3):604–6.

Blackburn, R. 1986. Patterns of personality deviation among violent offenders: Replication and extension of an empirical taxonomy. *British Journal of Criminology,* 26:254–69.

———. 1988. On moral judgements and personality disorders: The myth of psychopathic personality revisited. *British Journal of Psychiatry,* 153:505–12.

Blair, R. J., L. Jones, F. Clark, and M. Smith. 1997. The psychopathic individual: A lack of responsiveness to distress cues? *Psychophysiology,* 34:192–98.

Bock, G. R., and J. A. Goode. 1996. Genetics of criminal and antisocial behaviour. Ciba Foundation Symposium, 194. New York: Wiley.

Bradford, J. 1983. Research on sex offenders. *Psychiatric Clinics of North America,* 6:715–31.

Brennan, P., and S. Mednick. 1997. Medical histories of antisocial individuals. In D. Stoff, J. Breiling, and J. Maser (eds.), *Handbook of antisocial behavior.* New York: Wiley.

Brennan, P. A., E. R. Grekin, and S. A. Mednick. 1999. Maternal smoking during pregnancy and adult male criminal outcomes. *Archives of General Psychiatry,* 56(3):215–19.

Brennan, P.A., S. A. Mednick, and B. Jacobsen. 1996. Assessing the role of genetics in crime using adoption cohorts. Ciba Foundation Symposium, 194:115–23; discussion 123–28.

Brizer, D. A. 1988. Psychopharmacology and the management of violent patients. *Psychiatric Clinics of North America,* 11:551–68.

Brizer, D. A., and M. Crowner. 1989. *Current approaches to the prediction of violence.* Washington, D.C.: American Psychiatric Press.

Brooks-Gunn, J., C. McCarton, and T. Hawley. 1994. Effects of in utero drug exposure on children's development: Review and recommendations. *Archives of Pediatric and Adolescent Medicine,* 148:33–39.

Brown, G. L., M. H. Ebert, P. F. Goyer, D. C. Jimerson, W. J. Klein, W. E. Bunney, and F. K. Goodwin. 1982. Aggression, suicide, and serotonin: Relationship to CSF amine metabolites. *American Journal of Psychiatry,* 139:741–46.

Brown, G. L., F. K. Goodwin, J. C. Ballenger, P. F. Goyer, and L. F. Major. 1979. Aggression in humans correlates with cerebrospinal fluid amine metabolites. *Psychiatry Research,* 1:131–39.

Brunner, H. G. 1996. MAOA deficiency and abnormal behaviour: Perspectives on an association. In Ciba Foundation Symposium, Genetics of criminal and antisocial behaviour (pp. 155–67). Chichester: John Wiley & Sons.

Brunner, H. G., M. R. Nelen, X. O. Breakefield, H. H. Ropers, and B. A. van Oost. 1993b. Abnormal behavior associated with a point mutation in the structural gene for monoamine oxidase A. *Science,* 262:578–80.

Brunner, H. G., M. R. Nelen, P. van Zandvoort, N. G. Abeling, A. H. van Gennip, E. C. Wolters, M. A. Kuiper, H. H Ropers, and B. A. van Oost. 1993a. X-linked borderline mental retardation with prominent behavioral disturbance: Phenotype, genetic localization, and evidence for disturbed monoamine metabolism. *American Journal of Human Genetics,* 52:1032–39.

Buchsbaum, M. S., R. D. Coursey, and D. Murphy. 1976. The biochemical high-risk paradigm: Behavioral and familial correlates of low platelet monoamine oxidase activity. *Science,* 194(4262):339–41.

Buchsbaum, M. S., K. H. Nuechterlein, and R. J. Haier. 1990. Glucose metabolic rate in normals and schizophrenics during the continuous performance test assessed by positron emission tomography. *British Journal of Psychiatry,* 156:216–27.

Buikhuisen, W. 1987. Cerebral dysfunctions and persistent juvenile delinquency. In S. A. Mednick, T. E. Moffitt, and S. A. Stack (eds.), *The causes of crime: New biological approaches* (pp. 168–84). New York: Cambridge University Press.

Bushman, B. J., and R. G. Geen. 1992. Role of cognitive-emotional mediators and individual differences in the effects of media violence on aggression. *Journal of Personality and Social Psychology,* 58(1):156–63.

Buydens, B. L., and M. H. Branchey. 1992. Cortisol in alcoholics with a disordered aggression control. *Psychoneuroendocrinology,* 17:45–54.

Buydens-Branchey, L., D. Noumair, and C. S. Lieber. 1989. Age of alcohol onset: Relationship to susceptibility to serotonin precursor availability. *Archives of General Psychiatry,* 46:231–36.

Cadoret R. J., E. Troughton, T. W. O'Gorman, and E. Heywood. 1986. An adoption study of genetic and environmental factors in drug abuse. *Archives of General Psychiatry,* 43(12):1131–36.

Carey, G. 1992. Simulated twin data on substance abuse. *Behavioral Genetics,* 22(2):193–96.

———. 1995. Family and genetic epidemiology of aggressive and antisocial behavior. In D. M. Stoff and R. B. Cairns (eds.), *Aggression and violence: Genetic, neurobiological and biosocial perspectives* (pp. 3–21). Mahwah, NJ: Lawrence Erlbaum Assoc.

Carlson, N. R. 1994. *Physiology of behavior.* Boston: Allyn & Bacon.

Carruthers, M., and P. Taggart. 1973. Vagotonicity of violence: Biochemical and cardiac responses to violent films and television programmes. *British Medical Journal,* 3(876):384–89.

Cases, O., I. Seif, J. Grimsby, P. Gaspar, K. Chen, S. Pournin, U. Muller, M. Aguet, C. Babinet, J. C. Shih, and E. De Maeyer. 1995. Aggressive behavior and altered amounts of brain serotonin and norepinephrine in mice lacking MAOA. *Science,* 268:1763–66.

The Ciba Foundation Symposium. 1996. Genetics of criminal and antisocial behaviour. New York: John Wiley & Sons.

Cicchetti, D., F. A. Rogosch, S. L. Toth, and M. Spagnola. 1997. Affect, cognition and the emergency of self-knowledge in the toddler offspring of depressed mothers. *Journal of Experimental Child Psychology,* 67:338–62.

Cleckley, H. 1964. *The mask of sanity,* 4th ed. St. Louis: Mosby.

Cloninger, C. R. 1987. Neurogenetic adaptive mechanisms in alcoholism. *Science,* 236:410–16.

Cloninger, C. R., M. Bohman, and S. Sigvardsson. 1981. Inheritance of alcohol abuse: Cross-fostering analysis of adopted men. *Archives of General Psychiatry,* 38:861–68.

Cloninger, C. R., S. Sigvardsson, M. Bohman, and A-L. von Knorring. 1982. Predisposition to petty criminality in Swedish adoptees: II. Cross-fostering analysis of gene-environment interaction. *Archives of General Psychiatry,* 29:1242–47.

Coccaro, E. F., C. S. Bergeman, and G. E. McClearn. 1993. Heritability of irritable impulsiveness: A study of twins reared together and apart. *Psychiatric Research,* 48:229–42.

Coccaro, E., R. J., Kavoussi, and B. McNamee. 1999. Central neurotransmitter function in criminal aggression. In D. H. Fishbein (ed.), *The science, treatment and prevention of antisocial behavior.* New Jersey: Civic Research Institute.

Coccaro, E., and D. L. Murphy. 1991. *Serotonin in major psychiatric disorders.* Washington, D.C.: American Psychiatric Press, Inc.

Cohen, L. E., and R. Machalek, 1988. A general theory of expropriative crime: An evolutionary ecological approach. *American Journal of Sociology,* 94:465–501.

Comings, D. E. 1995. The role of genetic factors in conduct disorder based on studies of Tourette syndrome and ADHD probands and their relatives. *Journal of Development and Behavior in Pediatrics,* 16:142–57.

Comings, D. E., H. Wu, C. Chiu, R. H. Ring, G. Dietz, and D. Muhleman. 1996. Polygenic inheritance of Tourette syndrome, stuttering, ADHD, conduct and oppositional defiant disorder: The additive and subtractive effect of the three dopaminergic genes—DRD2, DbH and DAT1. *American Journal of Medical Genetics* (Neuropsychiatric Genetics), 67:264–88.

Cools, A. R., and M. A. Gingras. 1998. Nijmegen high and low responders to novelty: A new tool in the search after the neurobiology of drug abuse liability. *Pharmacology and Biochemistry of Behavior,* 60(1):151–59.

Cordoba, O. A., and J. L. Chapel. 1983. Medroxyprogesterone acetate antiandrogen treatment of hypersexuality in a pedophiliac sex offender. *American Journal of Psychiatry,* 140:1036–39.

Cozzoza, J. J., and H. J. Steadman. 1974. Some refinements in the measurement and prediction of dangerous behavior. *American Journal of Psychiatry,* 131:1012–14.

Dabbs, J. M., and M. F. Hargrove. 1997. Age, testosterone, and behavior among female prison inmates. *Psychosomatic Medicine,* 59:477–80.

Dabbs, J. M., R. B. Ruback, R. L. Frady, C. H. Hopper, and D. S. Sgoutas. 1988. Saliva testosterone and criminal violence among women. *Personality and Individual Differences,* 9:269–75.

Daly, M. 1996. Evolutionary adaptationism: Another biological approach to criminal and antisocial behaviour. In Ciba Foundation Symposium, Genetics of Criminal and Antisocial Behaviour, pp. 193–95. New York: John Wiley & Sons.

Damasio, H., T. Grabowski, R. Frank, A. M. Galaburda, and A. R. Damasio. 1994. The return of Phineas Gage: Clues about the brain from the skull of a famous patient. *Science,* 264:1102–4.

Damasio, A. R., D. Tranel, and H. Damasio. 1990. Individuals with sociopathic behavior caused by frontal damage fail to respond autonomically to social stimuli. *Behavioral Brain Research,* 41:81–94.

De Bellis, M. D., L. Burke, P. K. Trickett, and F. W. Putnam. 1996. Antinuclear antibodies and thyroid function in sexually abused girls. *Journal of Traumatic Stress,* 9(2):369–78.

De Bellis, M. D., G. P. Chrousos, L. D. Dorn, L. Burke, K. Helmers, M. A. Kling, P. K. Trickett, and F. W. Putnam. 1994. Hypothalamic-pituitary-adrenal axis dysregulation in sexually abused girls. *Journal of Clinical Endocrinology and Metabolism,* 78:249–55.

De Goeij, D. C., H. Dijkstra, and F. J. Tilders. 1991. Chronic psychosocial stress enhances vasopressin, but not corticotropin-releasing factor, in the external zone of the median eminence of male rats: Relationship to subordinate status. *Endocrinology,* 131(2):847–53.

Demsky, L. S. 1984. The use of Depo-Provera in the treatment of sex offenders. *The Journal of Legal Medicine,* 5:295–322.

Denno, D. 1990. *Biology and violence: From birth to adulthood.* Cambridge, MA: Cambridge University Press.

Devonshire, P. A., R. C. Howard, and C. Sellars. 1988. Frontal lobe functions and personality in mentally abnormal offenders. *Personality and Individual Differences,* 9:339–44.

Dinan, T. G. 1996. Serotonin: Current understanding and the way forward. *International Clinical Psychopharmacology,* 11 Suppl, 1:19–21.

Dolinski, Z. S., E. G. Shaskan, and M. N. Hesselbrock. 1985. Basic aspects of blood platelet monoamine oxidase activity in hospitalized men alcoholics. *Journal of Studies on Alcohol,* 46:81–85.

Dunn, et al., 1997. Maternal cigarette smoking during pregnancy and the child's subsequent development: II. Neurological and intellectual maturation to the age of 6½ years. *Canadian Journal of Public Health,* 68:43–50.

Edwards D. H., and E. A. Kravitz. 1997. Serotonin, social status and aggression. *Current Opinions in Neurobiology* 7(6):812–19. Review.

Eichelman, B. 1986. The biology and somatic experimental treatment of aggressive disorders. In P. A. Berger and H. K. H. Brodie (eds.), *The American handbook of psychiatry.* New York: Basic Books.

Elliott, D.S. 1994. Serious violent offenders: Onset, developmental course, and termination—The American Society of Criminology 1993 Presidential Address. *Criminology,* 32:1–21.

Elliott, F. 1977. Propranolol for the control of belligerent behavior following acute brain damage. *Annals of Neurology* 1:489–91.

———. 1992. Violence. The neurologic contribution: An overview. *Archives of Neurology,* 49:595–603.

Ellis, L. 1987. Criminal behavior and r/K selection: An extension of gene-based evolutionary theory. *Deviant Behavior,* 8:149–76.

———. 1987. Neurohormonal bases of varying tendencies to learn delinquent and criminal behavior. In E. Morris and C. Braukmann (eds.), *Behavioral approaches to crime and delinquency.* New York: Plenum.

————. 1989. Evolutionary and neurochemical causes of sex differences in victimizing behavior: Toward a unified theory of criminal behavior. *Social Science Information*, 28:605–36.

————. 1991. Monoamine oxidase and criminality: Identifying an apparent biological marker for antisocial behavior. *Journal of Research on Crime and Delinquency*, 28:227–51.

————. 1992. Monoamine oxidase and criminality: Identifying an apparent biological marker for antisocial behavior. *Journal of Research in Crime and Delinquency*, 28:227–51.

Ellis, L., and M. A. Ames. 1987. Neurohormonal functioning and sexual orientation: A theory of homosexuality-heterosexuality. *Psychological Bulletin*, 101(2):233–58.

Ellis, L., and A. Walsh. 1997. Gene-based evolutionary theories in criminology. *Criminology*, 35:229–76.

————. 2000. *Criminology: A global perspective*. Boston: Allyn & Bacon.

Evenden, J. L. 1999. Varieties of impulsivity. *Psychopharmacology*, 146:348–61.

Eysenck, H. J. 1977. *Crime and personality*. Rev. ed. London: Routledge & Kegan Paul.

Famy, C., A. P. Streissguth, and A. S. Unis. 1998. Mental illness in adults with fetal alcohol syndrome or fetal alcohol effects. *American Journal of Psychiatry*, 155:552–54.

Faraj, B. A., J. D. Lenton, M. Kutner, V. M. Camp, T. W. Stammers, S. R. Lee, P. A. Lolies, and D. Chandora. 1987. Prevalence of low monoamine oxidase function in alcoholism. *Alcoholism: Clinical and Experimental Research*, 11:464–67.

Farrington, D. P. 1987. Implications of biological findings for criminological research. In S. A. Mednick, T. E. Moffitt, and S. A. Stack (eds.), *The causes of crime: New biological approaches* (pp. 42–64). New York: Cambridge University Press.

Farrington, D. P. 1995. The development of offending and antisocial behaviour from childhood: Key findings from the Cambridge study in delinquent development. *Journal of Child Psychology*, 360:929–63.

Farrington, D. P., R. Loeber, and W. B. van Kammen. 1990. Long-term criminal outcomes of hyperactivity-impulsivity-attention deficit and conduct problems in childhood. In L. N. Robins and M. Rutter (eds.), *Straight and devious pathways from childhood to adult life* (pp. 62–81). Cambridge, England: Cambridge University Press.

Fava, M. 1999. Psychopharmacologic treatment of pathologic aggression. In D. H. Fishbein (ed.), *The science, treatment and prevention of antisocial behavior*. New Jersey: Civic Research Institute.

Fichtner, C. G., F. L. O'Connor, H. C. Yeoh, R. C. Arora, and J. W. Crayton. 1995. Hypodensity of platelet serotonin uptake sites in posttraumatic stress disorder: Associated clinical features. *Life Sciences*, 57(2):PL37–PL44.

Field, T. M., F. Scafidi, R. Pickens, M. Prodromidis, M. Pelaez-Nogueras, J. Torquati, H. Wilcox, J. Malphurs, J. Schanberg, and C. Kuhn. 1998. Polydrug-using adolescent mothers and their infants receiving early intervention. Adolescence, 33(129):117–43.

Finney J. W., and R. H. Moos. 1992. The long-term course of treated alcoholism: II. Predictors and correlates of 10-year functioning and mortality. J. Stud. Alcohol, 53(2):142–53.

Fishbein, D. H. 1990. Biological perspectives in criminology. *Criminology*, 18(1):27–73.

————. 1991. Medicalizing the drug war. *Behavioral Sciences and the Law*, 9:323–44.

————. 1992. The psychobiology of female aggression. *Criminal Justice and Behavior*, 19:99–126.

————. 1998. Differential susceptibility to comorbid drug abuse and violence. *Journal of Drug Issues*, 28(4):859–90.

————. 1999. *The science treatment and prevention of antisocial behavior: Applications to the criminal justice system*. New York: Civic Research Institute.

———. 2000. Sexual preference, crime and punishment. *Women and Criminal Justice*, 11(3):67–84.

Fishbein, D. H., and S. Pease. 1996. *The dynamics of drug abuse*. Boston: Allyn & Bacon.

Fishbein, D. H. and R. W. Thatcher. 1991. Legal applications of electrophysiological assessments. In J. Dywan, R. Kaplan, and F. Pirozzolo (eds.), *Neuropsychology and the law*. New York: Springer-Verlag, pp. 135–63.

Fishbein, D. H., D. Lozovsky, and J. H. Jaffe. 1989a. Impulsivity, aggressiveness and neuroendocrine responses to serotonergic stimulation in substance users. *Biological Psychiatry*, 25:1049–66.

Fishbein, D. H., R. I. Herning, W. B. Pickworth, C. A. Haertzen, J. E. Hickey, and J. H. Jaffe. 1989b. EEG and brainstem auditory evoked response potentials in adult male drug abusers with self-reported histories of aggressive behavior. *Biological Psychiatry*, 26:595–611.

Fogel C. A., S. A. Mednick, and N. Michelsen. 1985. Hyperactive behavior and minor physical anomalies. *Acta Psychiatrica Scandanavia*, Dec, 72(6):55–56.

Gabel, S., J. Stadler, J. Bjorn, R. Shindledecker, and C. J. Bowen. 1995. Homovanillic acid and monoamine oxidase in sons of substance-abusing fathers: Relationship to conduct disorders. *Journal of Studies on Alcohol*, 56:135–39.

Gerra, G., A. Zaimovic, G. Giucastro, F. Folli, D. Maestri, A. Tessoni, P. Avanzini, R. Caccavari, S. Bernasconi, and F. Brambilla. 1998. Neurotransmitter-hormonal responses to psychological stress in peripubertal subjects: Relationship to aggressive behavior. *Life Sciences*, 62(7):617–25

Gerra, G., R. Caccavari, R. Delsignore, M. Passeri, G. Fertonani Affini, D. Maestri, C. Monica, & F. Brambilla. 1993. Parental divorce and neuroendocrine changes in adolescents. Acta Psychiatrica Scandanavia, 87(5):350–54.

Giacoia, G. P. 1990. Cocaine in the cradle: A hidden epidemic. *Southern Medical Journal*, 83:947–51.

Giancola, P. R. 1995. Evidence for dorsolateral and orbital prefrontal cortical involvement in the expression of aggressive behavior. *Aggressive Behavior*, 21:431–50.

Giancola, P. R., H. B. Moss, C. S. Martin, L. Kirisci, and R. E. Tarter. 1996. Executive cognitive functioning predicts reactive aggression in boys at high risk for substance abuse: A prospective study. *Alcoholism: Clinical and Experimental Research*, 20:740–44.

Glantz, M. D., and R. W. Pickens. 1991. *Vulnerability to drug abuse. National Institute on Drug Abuse*, 1st ed. Washington, D.C.: American Psychological Association.

Glover, V. 1997. Maternal stress or anxiety in pregnancy and emotional development of the child. *British Journal of Psychiatry*, 171:105–6.

Goldman, D. 1993. Recent developments in alcoholism: Genetic transmission. *Recent Developments in Alcoholism*, 11:231–48. Review.

Goldman, D., J. Lappalainen, and N. Ozaki. 1996. Direct analysis of candidates genes in impulsive behaviors. Ciba Foundation Symposium, 194:139–52.

Goodman, S. H., and I. H. Gotlib. 1999. Risk for psychopathology in the children of depressed mothers: A developmental model for understanding mechanisms of transmission. *Psychology Review*, 106:458–90.

Gorio, A., E. Germani, P. Mantegazza, A. M. Di Giulio, and A. Bertelli. 1992. Perinatal exposure to ethanol affects postnatal degeneration and regeneration of serotonergic pathways in the spinal cord. *Drugs Experimental and Clinical Research*, 18:461–64.

Gottesman, I. I., and H. H. Goldsmith. 1994. Developmental psychopathology of antisocial behavior: Inserting genes into its ontogenesis and epigenesis. In C. A. Nelson (ed.), *Threats to optimal development: Integrating biological, psychological, and social risk factors* (pp. 69–104). Hillsdale, NJ: Lawrence Erlbaum Assoc.

Gottesman, I. I., and J. Shields. 1982. The epigenetic puzzle. Cambridge: Cambridge University Press.

Gottfredson, S. 1986. Statistical and actual considerations. In F. Dutile and C. Foust (eds.), *The prediction of criminal violence*. Springfield, IL: Charles C. Thomas.

Goyer, P. F., P. J. Andreason, W. E. Semple, A. H. Clayton, A. C. King, B. A. Compton-Toth, S. C. Schultz, and R. M. Cohen. 1994. Positron-emission tomography and personality disorders. *Neuropsychopharmacology*, 10:21–28.

Graeff, F. G., F. S. Guimaraes, T. G. De Andrade, & J. F. Deakin. 1996. Role of 5-HT in stress, anxiety, and depression. *Pharmacology and Biochemistry of Behavior*, 54(1):129–41.

Gray, J. A. 1983. A theory of anxiety: The role of the limbic system. *Encephale*, 9(4 Suppl 2), 161B–166B.

Gray, J. A., and N. McNaughton. 1983. Comparison between the behavioural effects of septal and hippocampal lesions: A review. *Neuroscience Biobehavioral Review*, 7(2):119–88.

Groer, M., and M. Howell. 1990. Autonomic and cardiovascular responses of preschool children to television programs. *Journal of Child and Adolescent Psychiatric and Mental Health Nursing*, 3(4):134–38.

Guerri, G., A. Zaimovic, G. Giucastro, F. Folli, D. Maestri, A. Tessoni, P. Avanzini, R. Caccavari, S. Bernasconi, and F. Brambilla. 1998. Neurotransmitter-hormonal responses to psychological stress in peripubertal subjects: Relationship to aggressive behavior. *Life Sciences*, 62:617–25.

Gunnar, M. R., K. Tout, M. de Haan, S. Pierce, and K. Stansbury. 1997. Temperament, social competence, and adrenocortical activity in preschoolers. *Developmental Psychobiology*, 31(1):65–85.

Gust, D. A., T. P. Gordon, M. E. Wilson, A. Ahmed-Ansari, A. R. Brodie, and H. M. McClure. 1991. Formation of a new social group of unfamiliar female rhesus monkeys affects the immune and pituitary adrenocortical systems. *Brain and Behavioral Immunology*, 5:296–307.

Hare, R. 1984. Performance of psychopaths on cognitive tasks related to frontal lobe function. *Journal of Abnormal Psychology*, 93:141–49.

Hare, R., and D. Schalling. 1978. *Psychopathic behaviour*. New York: John Wiley & Sons.

Hauser, P., A. J. Zametkin, P. Martinez, B. Vitiello, J. A. Matochik, A. J. Mixson, and B. D. Weintraub. 1993. Attention deficit-hyperactivity disorder in people with generalized resistance to thyroid hormone. *New England Journal of Medicine*, 328:997–1001.

Hawkins, D. 1989. Intentional injury: Are there no solutions? *Law Medicine and Health Care* 17:32–41.

Hazzlett, E., M. Dawson, M. S. Buchsbaum, and K. Neuchterlein. 1993. Reduced regional brain glucose metabolism assessed by PET in electrodermal nonresponder schizophrenics: A pilot study. *Journal of Abnormal Psychology*, 102:39–46.

Henry, C., G. Guegant, M. Cador, E. Arnauld, J. Arsaut, M. LeMoal, and J. Demotes-Mainard. 1995. Prenatal stress in rats facilitates amphetamine-induced sensitization and induces long-lasting changes in dopamine receptors in the nucleus accumbens. *Brain Research*, 685:179–86.

Higley, J. D., P. T. Mehlman, R. E. Poland, D. M. Taub, J. Vickers, S. J. Suomi, and M. Linnoila. 1996. CSF testosterone and 5-HIAA correlate with different types of aggressive behaviors. *Biological Psychiatry*, 40:1067–82.

Higley, J. D., S. J. Suomi, and M. Linnoila. 1991. CSF monoamine metabolite concentrations vary according to age, rearing, and sex, and are influenced by the stressor of social separation in rhesus monkeys. *Psychopharmacology* (Berl), 103(4):551–56.

Hillbrand, M., and N. J. Pallone. 1993. *The psychobiology of aggression: Engines, measurement, control.* New York: The Haworth Press.

Hofkosh, D., J. L. Pringle, H. P. Wald, J. Switala. 1995. Early interactions between drug-involved mothers and infants: Within-group differences. *Archives of Pediatric and Adolescent Medicine,* 149:665–72.

Holsboer, F. 1989. Psychiatric implications of altered limbic-hypothalamic-pituitary-adrenocortical activity. *European Archives of Psychiatry and Neurological Sciences,* 238(5–6):302–22.

Horger, B. A., and R. H. Roth. 1996. The role of mesoprefrontal dopamine neurons in stress. *Critical Reviews in Neurobiology,* 10(3–4):395–418.

Howard, R. C. 1986. Psychopathy: A psychobiological perspective. *Personality and Individual Differences,* 7:795–806.

Howard, S. G., and H. Takeda. 1990. Effect of prenatal exposure to phencyclidine on the postnatal development of the cholinergic system in the rat. *Developmental Neuroscience,* 12:204–9.

Hsu, Y-PP, J. F. Powell, K. B. Sims, and X. O. Breakefield. 1989. Molecular genetics of the monoamine oxidases. *Journal of Neurochemistry,* 53:12–18.

Hurt, J., and J. A. Naglieri. 1992. Performance of delinquent and nondelinquent males on planning, attention, simultaneous, and successful cognitive processing tasks. *Journal of Clinical Psychology,* 46:120–28.

Hussong A. M., and L. Chassin. 1997. Substance use initiation among adolescent children of alcoholics: Testing protective factors. *Journal on Studies of Alcohol,* 58(3):272–79.

Jeffery, C. R. 1985. Attacks on the insanity defense: Biological psychiatry and new perspectives on criminal behavior. Springfield, IL: Charles C. Thomas.

Ito, Y., M. H. Teicher, C. A. Glod, and E. Ackerman. 1998. Preliminary evidence for aberrant cortical development in abused children: A quantitative EEG study. *Journal of Neuropsychiatry and Clinical Neuroscience,* 10(3):298–307.

Ito, Y., M. H. Teicher, C. A. Glod, D. Harper, E. Magnus, and H. A. Gelbard. 1993. Increased prevalence of electrophysiological abnormalities in children with psychological, physical, and sexual abuse. *Journal of Neuropsychiatry and Clinical Neuroscience,* 5(4):401–8.

Kagan, J. 1992. Behavior, biology, and the meanings of temperamental constructs. *Pediatrics,* 90(3 Pt 2):510–13.

Kagan J., J. S. Reznick, and N. Snidman. 1988. Biological basis of childhood shyness. *Science,* 240(4849):167–71.

Kalamas A. D., and M. L. Gruber. 1998. Electrodermal responses to implied versus actual violence on television. *Journal of General Psychology,* 125(1):31–37.

Kandel, E., P. A. Brennan, S. A. Mednick, and N. M. Michelson. 1989. Minor physical anomalies and recidivistic adult violent criminal behavior. *Acta Psychiatrica Scandanavia,* 79(1):103–7.

Kandel, E., and D. Freed. 1989. Frontal-lobe dysfunction and antisocial behavior: A review. *Journal of Clinical Psychology,* 45:404–13.

Kaufer, D., A. Friedman, S. Seidman, and H. Soreq. 1998. Acute stress facilitates long-lasting changes in cholinergic gene expression. *Nature,* 393:373–77.

Kaufman, J., B. Birmaher, J. Perel, R. E. Dahl, P. Moreci, B. Nelson, W. Wells, and N. D. Ryan. 1997. The corticotropin-releasing hormone challenge in depressed abused, depressed nonabused, and normal control children. *Biological Psychiatry,* 42:669–79.

Kelley, B. T., R. Loeber, K. Keenan, and M. DeLamatre. 1997. Development pathways in boys' disruptive and delinquent behavior. *Juvenile Justice Bulletin,* OJJDP. Washington, D.C.: U.S. Department of Justice.

Kempermann, G., H. G. Kuhn, and F. H. Gage. 1998. Experience-induced neurogenesis in the senescent dentate gyrus. *Journal of Neuroscience,* 18(9):3206–12.

Kittrie, N. 1971. *The right to be different: Deviance and enforced therapy.* Baltimore, MD: Johns Hopkins University Press.

Kouri, E. M., S. E. Lukas, H. G. Pope, Jr., and P. S. Oliva. 1995. Increased aggressive responding in male volunteers following the administration of gradually increasing doses of testosterone cypionate. *Drug and Alcohol Dependence,* 40:73–79.

Kraemer, G. W., M. H. Ebert, D. E. Schmidt, and W. T. McKinney. 1989. A longitudinal study of the effect of different social rearing conditions on cerebrospinal fluid norepinephrine and biogenic amine metabolites in rhesus monkeys. *Neuropsychopharmacology,* 2(3):175–89.

Kruesi, M. J. P., E. Hibbs, T. Zahn, C. S. Keysor, S. D. Hamburger, J. J. Bartko, and J. L. Rapaport. 1992. A 2-year prospective follow-up study of children and adolescents with disruptive behavior disorders: Prediction by CSF 5HIAA, HVA, and autonomic measures? *Archives of General Psychiatry,* 49:429–35.

Kuhn, C. M., and S. M. Schanberg. 1998. Responses to maternal separation: Mechanisms and mediators. *International Journal of Developmental Neuroscience,* 16:261–70.

Lappalainen, J., J. C. Long, M. Eggert, N. Ozaki, R. W. Robin, G. L. Brown, H. Naukkarinen, M. Virkkunen, M. Linnoila, and D. Goldman. 1998. Linkage of antisocial alcoholism to the serotonin 5-HT1B receptor gene in 2 populations. *Archives of General Psychiatry.* Nov, 55(11):989–94.

Legido, A. 1997. Intrauterine exposure to drugs. *Reviews in Neurology,* 25:691–702.

Lemieux, A. M., and C. L. Coe. 1995. Abuse-related posttraumatic stress disorder: Evidence for chronic neuroendocrine activation in women. *Psychosomatic Medicine,* 57:105–15.

Lewis, D. O. 1992. From abuse to violence: Psychophysiological consequences of maltreatment. *Journal of the American Academy of Child and Adolescent Psychiatry,* 31:383–91.

Lidberg, L., I. Modin, L. Oreland, J. R. Tuck, and A. Gillner. 1985. Platelet monoamine oxidase activity and psychopathy. *Psychiatry Research,* 16:339–43.

Linnoila, M., M. Virkkunen, M. Eckardt, J. D. Higley, D. Nielsen, and D. Goldman. 1994. Serotonin, violent behavior and alcohol. *EXS,* 71:155–63.

Linnoila, M., M. Virkkunen, M. Scheinin, A. Nuutila, R. Rimon, and F. K. Goodwin. 1982. Low CSF 5HIAA concentration differentiates impulsive from nonimpulsive violent behavior. *Life Sciences,* 33:2609–14.

Linnoila, M., M. Virkkunen, M. Scheinin, A. Nuutila, R. Rimon, and F. K. Goodwin. 1983. Low cerebrospinal fluid 5-hydroxyindoleacetic acid concentration differentiates impulsive from nonimpulsive violent behavior. *Life Sciences,* 33(26):2609–14.

Loeber, R., and M. LeBlanc. 1991. Toward a developmental criminology. In M. Tonry and N. Morris (eds.), *Crime and justice* (pp. 375–473). Chicago: The University of Chicago Press.

Loeber, R., and M. Stouthamer-Loeber. 1998. Development of juvenile aggression and violence. Some common misconceptions and controversies. *American Psychologist,* 53:242–59.

Lou, H. C., D. Hansen, and M. Nordenfoft. 1994. Prenatal stressors of human life affect fetal brain development. *Developmental Medicine and Child Neurology,* 36:826–32.

Lueger, R. J., and K. F. Gill. 1990. Frontal-lobe cognitive dysfunction in conduct disorder adolescents. *Journal of Clinical Psychology,* 46:696–705.

Magnusson, D. 1987. Adult delinquency in the light of conduct and physiology at an early age: A longitudinal study. In D. Magnusson and A. Ohman (eds.), *Psychopathology: An international perspective.* Orlando, FL: Academic Press.

Magnusson, D. 1988. *Individual development from an interactional perspective: A longitudinal study.* Hillsdale, NJ: Lawrence Erlbaum Associates.

Marsh, F. H., and J. Katz. 1985. *Biology, crime and ethics: A study of biological explanations for criminal behavior.* Cincinnati: Anderson Publishing.

Marx, G. 1985. I'll be watching you. *Dissent* (Winter):6–34.

Maxfield, M. G., and C. S. Widom. 1996. The cycle of violence. Revisited 6 years later. *Archives of Pediatric and Adolescent Medicine*, 150(4):390–95.

Mayes, L. C., R. H. Granger, M. A. Frank, R. Schottenfeld, and M. H. Bornstein. 1993. Neurobehavioral profiles of neonates exposed to cocaine prenatally. *Pediatrics*, 91:778–83.

Mazur, A., and A. Booth. 1998. Testosterone and dominance in men. *Behavior and Brain Sciences*, 21:353–63.

McEwen, B. S. 1997. Possible mechanisms for atrophy of the human hippocampus. *Molecular Psychiatry*, 2:255–62.

McEwen, B. S., D. Albeck, H. Cameron, H. M. Chao, E. Gould, N. Hastings, Y. Kuroda, V. Luine, A. M. Magarinos, and C. R. McKittrick. 1995. Stress and the brain: A paradoxical role for adrenal steroids. *Vitamins and Hormones*, 51:371–402.

McIntosh, D. E., R. S. Mulkins, and R. S. Dean. 1995. Utilization of maternal perinatal risk indicators in the differential diagnosis of ADHD and ADD children. *International Journal of Neuroscience*, 81:35–46.

Mealey, L. 1995. The sociobiology of sociopathy: An integrated evolutionary model. *Behavioral and Brain Sciences*, 18:523–99.

Meaney, M. J., and D. H. Aitken. 1985. The effects of early postnatal handling on hippocampal glucocorticoid receptor concentrations: Temporal parameters. *Brain Research*, 354:301–4.

Meaney, M. J., J. Diorio, D. Francis, J. Widdowson, P. LaPlante, C. Caldji, S. Sharma, J. R. Seckl, and P. M. Plotsky. 1996. Early environmental regulation of forebrain glucocorticoid receptor gene expression: Implications for adrenocortical responses to stress. *Developmental Neuroscience*, 18(1–2):49–72.

Meaney, M. J., J. B. Mitchell, D. H. Aitken, S. Bhatnagar, S. R. Bodnoff, L. J. Iny, and A. Sarrieau. 1991. The effects of neonatal handling on the development of the adrenocortical response to stress: Implications for neuropathology and cognitive deficits in later life. *Psychoneuroendocrinology*, 16:85–103.

Mednick, S. A., and E. S. Kandel. 1988. Congenital determinants of violence. *Bulletin of the American Academy of Psychiatry Law*, 16(2):101–9.

Mednick S. A., T. E. Moffitt, and S. A. Stack. 1987. *The causes of crime: New biological approaches.* New York: Cambridge University Press.

Miczek, K. A., A. F. Mirsky, G. Carey, J. DeBold, and A. Raine. 1994. An overview of biological influences on violent behavior. *Understanding and preventing violence*, Vol. 2, Biobehavioral Influences. National Research Council: Washington, D.C.

Milberger, S., J. Biederman, S. V. Faraone, L. Chen, and J. Jones. 1996. Is maternal smoking during pregnancy a risk factor for attention deficit hyperactivity disorder in children? *American Journal of Psychiatry*, 153:1138–42.

Milberger, S., J. Biederman, S. V. Faraone, L. Chen, and J. Jones. 1997. Further evidence of an association between attention-deficit/hyperactivity disorder and cigarette smoking. Findings from a high-risk sample of siblings. *American Journal of Addiction*, 6:205–17.

Milner, J. S. (ed.). 1991. *Neuropsychology of aggression.* Boston: Kluwer.

Mirkin, A. M., and A. Coppen. 1980. Electrodermal activity in depression: Clinical and biochemical correlates. *British Journal of Psychiatry*, 137:93–97.

Mirsky, A. F., and A. Siegel. 1994. The neurobiology of violence and aggression. In A. J. Reiss, Jr., K. A. Miczek, and J. A. Roth (eds.), *Violence: Biobehavioral influences*, (Vol. 2, pp. 59–172), Washington D.C.: National Academy Press.

Moffitt, T. E. 1990. Juvenile delinquency and attention deficit disorder: Boys' developmental trajectories from age 3 to age 15. *Child Development,* 61(3):893–910.

Moffitt, T. E., S. A. Mednick, and W. F. Gabrielli, Jr. 1989. Predicting careers of criminal violence: Descriptive data and predispositional factors. In D. A. Brizer, and M. Crowner (eds.), Current Approaches to the Prediction of Violence. Washington, D.C.: *American Psychiatric Press.*

Moffitt, T. E. 1993. Adolescence-limited and life-course-persistent antisocial behavior: A developmental taxonomy. *Psychology Review,* 100(4):674–701. Review.

Moffitt, T. E. 1997. Neuropsychology, antisocial behavior, and neighborhood context. In J. McCord (ed.), *Violence and child in the inner city.* Cambridge: Cambridge University Press.

Moffitt, T. E., A. Caspi, A. R. Harkness, & P. A. Silva. 1993. The natural history of change in intellectual performance: who changes? How much? Is it meaningful? Journal of Child Psychology and Psychiatry, 34(4):455–506.

Moffitt, T. E., G. L. Brammer, A. Caspi, J. P. Fawcett, M. Raleigh, A. Yuwiler, and P. Silva. 1997. Whole blood serotonin relates to violence in an epidemiological study. *Biological Psychiatry,* 15, 43(6):446–57.

Monahan, J. 1981. *The clinical prediction of violent behavior.* Rockville, MD: U.S. Department of Health and Human Services.

Moss, H. B., J. K. Yao, and G. L. Panzak. 1990. Serotonergic responsivity and behavioral dimensions in antisocial personality disorder with substance abuse. *Biological Psychiatry,* 28:325–38.

Mott, S. H., R. J. Packer, and S. J. Soldin. 1993. Neurologic manifestations of cocaine exposure in childhood. *Pediatrics,* 92:557–60.

Muhlbauer, H. D. 1985. Human aggression and the role of central serotonin. *Pharmacopsychiatry,* 18:218–21.

Murray, J. B. 1987. Psychopharmacological therapy of deviant sexual behavior. *Journal of General Psychology,* 115:101–10.

Nagin, D. S., and D. P. Farrington. 1992. The stability of criminal potential from childhood to adulthood. *Criminology,* 30:235–60.

Neihoff, D. 1999. *The biology of violence.* New York: Free Press.

Newman, J. P. 1987. Reaction to punishment in extroverts and psychopaths: Implications for the impulsive behavior of disinhibited individuals. *Journal of Research in Personality,* 21:464–80.

Niskanen, P., and K. A. Achte. 1972. The course and prognoses of schizophrenic psychoses in Helsinki: A comparative study of first admissions in 1950, 1960 and 1965. Monograph of Psychiatric Clinics in Helsinki. University Central Hospital.

Nyborg, H. 1984. Performance and intelligence in hormonally different groups. *Progress in Brain Research,* 61:491–508.

Oates, R. K., D. Forrest, and A. Peacock. 1985. Self-esteem of abused children. *Child Abuse and Neglect,* 9:159–63.

O'Connor, T. G., K. Deater-Deckard, D. Fulker, M. Rutter, and R. Plomin. 1998b. Genotype-environment correlations in late childhood and early adolescence: Antisocial behavioral problems and coercive parenting. *Developmental Psychology,* 34:970–81.

O'Connor, T. G., S. McGuire, D. Reiss, E. M. Hetherington, and R. Plomin. 1998a. Co-occurrence of depressive symptoms and antisocial behavior in adolescence: A common genetic liability. *Journal of Abnormal Psychology,* 107(1):27–37.

Oreland, L., L. von Knorring, and D. Schalling. 1983. Connections between monoamine oxidase, temperament and disease. In W. Patton, J. Mitchell, and P. Turner (eds.), *Proceedings of the IXth International Congress of Pharmacology,* Vol. 2. London: Macmillan.

Orlebeke, J. F., D. L. Knol., and F. C. Verhulst. 1997. Increase in child behavior problems resulting from maternal smoking during pregnancy. *Archives of Environmental Health,* 52:317–21.

Osborn, D. K., and R. C. Endsley. 1971. Emotional reactions of young children to TV violence. *Child Development,* 42(1):321–31.

Pallone, N. J., and J. J. Hennessy. 1996. *Tinder box criminal aggression: Neuropsychology, demography, phenomenology.* New Jersey: Transaction Publishers.

Patterson, G. R., B. D. DeBaryshe, and E. Ramsey. 1989. Developmental perspective on antisocial behavior. *American Psychologist,* 44(2):329–35.

Pennington, B. F., and L. Bennetto. 1993. Main effects or transactions in the neuropsychology of conduct disorder? Commentary on "The neuropsychology of conduct disorder." *Development and Psychopathology 5,* 153–64.

Petty, F., L. L. Davis, D. Kabel, & G. L. Kramer. 1996. Serotonin dysfunction disorders: A behavioral neurochemistry perspective. *Journal of Clinical Psychiatry,* 57 Suppl 8:11–16.

Phillips, T. J., A. J. Roberts, and C. N. Lessov. 1997. Behavioral sensitization to ethanol: Genetics and the effects of stress. *Pharmacology and Biochemistry of Behavior,* 57:487–93.

Piazza, P. V., and M. L. Le Moal. 1996. Pathophysiological basis of vulnerability to drug abuse: Role of an interaction between stress, glucocorticoids and dopaminergic neurons. *Annual Reviews in Pharmacology and Toxicology,* 36:359–78.

Piazza, P. V., and M. L. Le Moal. 1998. The role of stress in drug self-administration. *Trends in the Pharmacological Sciences,* 19:67–74.

Pihl, R. O. and J. B. Petersen. 1995. Alcoholism: The role of different motivational systems. *Journal of Psychiatry and Neuroscience,* 20:372–96.

Pincus, J., and G. Tucker. 1974. *Behavioral neurology.* New York: Oxford University Press.

Pine, D. S., J. D. Coplan, G. A. Wasserman, L. S. Miller, J. E. Fried, M. Davies, T. B. Cooper, L. Greenhill, D. Shaffer, and B. Parsons. 1997. Neuroendocrine response to fenfluramine challenge in boys. Associations with aggressive behavior and adverse rearing. *Archives of General Psychiatry,* 54(9):839–46.

Pine, D. S., G. A. Wasserman, J. Coplan, J. A. Fried, Y. Y. Huang, S. Kassir, L. Greenhill, D. Shaffer, and B. Parsons. 1996. Platelet serotonin 2A (5-HT2A) receptor characteristics and parenting factors for boys at risk for delinquency: A preliminary report. *American Journal of Psychiatry,* 153(4):538–44.

Piquero, A., and S. G. Tibbetts. 1999. The impact of pre/perinatal disturbances and disadvantaged familial environment in predicting criminal offending. *Studies on Crime and Crime Prevention,* 8(1):52–70.

Plomin, R., and D. Daniels. 1987. Why are children in the same family so different from one another? *Behavioral and Brain Sciences,* 10:1–16.

Pomeroy, J. C., J. Sprafkin, and K. D. Gadow. 1988. Minor physical anomalies as a biologic marker for behavior disorders. *Journal of the American Academy of Child and Adolescent Psychiatry,* Jul, 27(4):466–73.

Post, R. M. 1992. Transduction of psychosocial stress into the neurobiology of recurrent affective disorder. *American Journal of Psychiatry,* 149:999–1010.

Post, R. M., and S. R. Weiss. 1997. Emergent properties of neural systems: How focal molecular neurobiological alterations can affect behavior. *Developmental Psychopathology,* 9(4):907–29.

Power C., and V. Estaugh. 1990. The role of family formation and dissolution in shaping drinking behaviour in early adulthood. *British Journal of Addiction,* 85(4):521–30.

Quay, H. C. 1987. Patterns of delinquent behavior. In H. C. Quay (ed.), *Handbook of juvenile delinquency.* (pp. 119–38). New York: John Wiley & Sons.

Raine, A. 1988. Psychopathy: A single or dual concept? *Personality and Individual Differences,* 9(4):825–27.

Raine, A. 1993. *The psychopathology of crime: Criminal behavior as a clinical disorder.* New York: Academic Press.

Raine, A., P. Brennan, & S. A. Mednick. 1994. Birth complications combined with early maternal rejection at age 1 year predispose to violent crime at age 18 years. *Archives of General Psychiatry,* 51(12):984–8.

Raine, A., P. A. Brennan, D. P. Farrington, and S. A. Mednick. 1997a. *Biosocial bases of violence.* New York: Plenum Press.

Raine, A., M. Buchsbaum, and L. LaCasse. 1997c. Brain abnormalities in murderers indicated by positron emission tomography. *Biological Psychiatry,* 42:495–508

Raine, A., M. S. Buchsbaum, J. Stanley, S. Lottenberg, L. Abel., and S. Stoddard. 1993. Selective reductions in prefrontal glucose metabolism in murderers. *Biological Psychiatry,* 36:365–73.

Raine, A., and J. Liu. 1998. Biological predispositions to violence and their implications for biosocial treatment and prevention. *Psychology, Crime and Law,* 4:107–25.

Raine, A., G. P. Reynolds, and C. Sheard. 1991. Neuroanatomical correlates of skin conductance orienting in normal humans: A magnetic resonance imaging study. *Psychophysiology,* 28(5):548–58.

Raine, A., P. H. Venables, and S. A. Mednick. 1997b. Reduced resting heart rate at age 3 years predicts to aggressive behavior at age 11 years: Findings from the Mauritius Child Health Study. *Journal of the American Academy of Child and Adolescent Psychiatry,* 36(10):1457–64.

Raine, A., P. H. Venables, and M. Williams. 1990. Relationships between CNS and ANS measures of arousal at age 15 and criminality at age 24. *Archives of General Psychiatry,* 47:1003–7.

Raleigh, M. J., M. T. McGuire, G. L. Brammer, D. B. Pollack, & A. Yuwiler. 1991. Serotonergic mechanisms promote dominance acquisition in adult male vervet monkeys. *Brain Research,* 559(2):181–90.

Rampling, D. 1978. Aggression: A paradoxical response to tricyclic antidepressants. *American Journal of Psychiatry,* 135:117–18.

Rantakallio, P., E. Laara, M. Isohanni, and I. Moilanen. 1992. Maternal smoking during pregnancy and delinquency of the offspring: An association without causation? *International Journal of Epidemiology,* 21:1106–13.

Ratey, J. J., E. J. Mikkelsen, G. B. Smith, A. Upadhyaya, H. S. Zuckerman, D. Martell, P. Sorgi, S. Polakoff, and J. Bemporad. 1986. Beta-blockers in the severely and profoundly mentally retarded. *Journal of Clinical Psychopharmacology,* 6:103–7.

Ratey, J. J., E. J. Mikkelsen, P. Sorgi, H. S. Zuckerman, S. Polakoff, J. Bemporad, P. Bick, and W. Kadish. 1987. Autism: The treatment of aggressive behaviors. *Journal of Clinical Psychopharmacology,* 7:35–41.

Reiss, A. J., Jr., K. A. Miczek, and J. A. Roth. 1994. *Understanding and preventing violence.* Volume 2. Biobehavioral Influences. Washington, D.C.: National Academy Press.

Reiss, A. J., and J. A. Roth (eds.). 1993. *Understanding and preventing violence.* Washington, D.C.: National Academy Press.

Rosenberg, M. L., and J. A. Mercy. 1986. Homicide: Epidemiologic analysis at the national level. *Bulletin of the New York Academy of Medicine,* 62(5):376–99.

Rosenblum, L. A., and M. W. Andrews. 1994. Influences of environmental demand on maternal behavior and infant development. *Acta Paediatrica Supplement,* 397:57–63.

Rosenfeld, R., and S. Decker. 1993. Where public health and law enforcement meet: Monitoring and preventing youth violence. *American Journal of Police,* 12:11–57.

Roughton, E. C., M. L. Schneider, L. J. Bromley, and C. L. Coe. 1998. Maternal endocrine activation during pregnancy alters neurobehavioral state in primate infants. *American Journal of Occupational Therapy,* 52:90–98.

Rowe, D. C. 1983. Biometrical genetic models of self-reported delinquent behavior: A twin study. *Behavioral Genetics,* 13(5):473–89.

Rowe, D. C. 1986. Genetic and environmental components of antisocial behavior: A study of 265 twin pairs. *Criminology,* 24(3):513–32.

Rowe, D. C., C. Stever, J. M. Gard, H. H. Cleveland, M. L. Sanders, A. Abramowitz, S. T. Kozol, J. H. Mohr, S. L. Sherman, and I. D. Waldman. 1998a. The relation of the dopamine transporter gene (DAT1) to symptoms of internalizing disorders in children. *Behavioral Genetics,* 28(3):215–25.

Rowe, D. C., C. Stever, L. N. Giedinghagen, J. M. C. Gard, H. Cleveland, S. T. Terris, J. H. Mohr, S. Sherman, A. Abramowitz, and I. D. Waldman. 1998b. Dopamine DRD4 receptor polymorphism and attention deficit hyperactivity disorder. *Molecular Psychiatry,* 3:419–26.

Roy, A., M. Virkkunen, and M. Linnoila. 1987. Reduced central serotonin turnover in a subgroup of alcoholics. Progress in Neuropsychopharmacology. *Biological Psychiatry,* 11:173–77.

Rubinow, D. R., and P. J. Schmidt. 1996. Androgens, brain, and behavior. *American Journal of Psychiatry,* 153(8):974–84.

Rushton, J. P. 1990. Race and crime: A reply to Roberts and Gabor. *Canadian Journal of Criminology,* 32:315–34.

Rushton, J. P. 1995. Race and crime: International data for 1989–1990. *Psychological Reports,* 76:307–12.

Ryan, N. D. 1988. Psychoneuroendocrinology of children and adolescents. *Psychiatric Clinics of North America,* 21(2):435–41.

Sapolsky, R. M. 1989. Hypercortisolism among socially subordinate wild baboons originates at the CNS level. *Archives of General Psychiatry,* 46(11):1047–51.

Sapolsky, R. M. 1996. Why stress is bad for your brain. *Science,* 273(5276):749–50.

Sapolsky, R. M., and G. E. Mott. 1987. Social subordinance in wild baboons is associated with suppressed high density lipoprotein-cholesterol concentrations: The possible role of chronic social stress. *Endocrinology,* 121(5):1605–10.

Schalling, D. 1993. Neurochemical correlates of personality, impulsivity, and disinhibitory suicidality. In S. Hodgins (eds.), *Mental disorder and crime* (pp. 208–26). Newbury Park, CA: Sage.

Schalling, D., M. Asberg, G. Edman, and L. Oreland. 1987. Markers for vulnerability to psychopathology: Temperament traits associated with platelet MAO activity. *Acta Psychiatrica Scandanavia,* 76(2):172–82.

Schmidt, L. A., and N. A. Fox. 1994. Patterns of cortical electrophysiology and autonomic activity in adults' shyness and sociability. *Biological Psychology,* 38(2–3):183–98.

Schmidt L. A., N. A. Fox, K. H. Rubin, E. M. Sternberg, P. W., Gold, C. C. Smith, and J. Schulkin. 1997. Behavioral and neuroendocrine responses in shy children. *Developmental Psychobiology,* 30(2):127–40.

Seguin, J. R., R. O. Pihl, P. W. Harden, R. E. Tremblay, and B. Boulerice. 1995. Cognitive and neuropsychological characteristics of physically aggressive boys. *Journal of Abnormal Psychology,* 104:614–24.

Seidler, F. J., and T. A. Slotkin. 1992. Fetal cocaine exposure causes persistent noradrenergic hyperactivity in rat brain regions: Effects on neurotransmitter turnover and receptors. *Journal of Pharmacology and Experimental Therapeutics,* 263:413–21.

Senba, E., and T. Ueyama. 1997. Stress-induced expression of immediate early genes in the brain and peripheral organs of the rat. *Neuroscience Research,* 29:183–207.

Shapiro, S. K., H. C. Quay, A. E. Hogan, and K. P. Schwartz. 1988. Response perseveration and delayed responding in undersocialized aggressive conduct disorder. *Journal of Abnormal Psychology,* 97:371–273.

Shin, L. M., R. J. McNally, S. M. Kosslyn, W. L. Thompson, S. L. Rauch, N. M. Alpert, L. J. Metzger, N. B. Lasko, S. P. Orr, and R. K. Pitman. 1997. A positron emission tomographic study of symptom provocation in PTSD. *Annals of the New York Academy of Sciences,* 821:521–23.

Siegel, S. J., S. D. Ginsberg, P. R. Hof, S. L. Foote, W. G. Young, G. W. Kraemer, W. T. McKinney, and J. H. Morrison. 1993. Effects of social deprivation in prepubescent rhesus monkeys: Immunohistochemical analysis of the neurofilament protein triplet in the hippocampal formation. *Brain Research,* 619(1–2):299–305.

Simon, N. G., and R. E. Whalen. 1986. Hormonal regulation of aggression: Evidence for a relationship among genotype, receptor binding, and behavioral sensitivity to androgen and estrogen. *Aggressive Behavior,* 12:255–66.

Slotkin, T. A. 1998. Fetal nicotine or cocaine exposure: Which one is worse? *Journal of Pharmacology and Experimental Therapeutics,* 285:931–45.

Smith, M. A. 1996. Hippocampal vulnerability to stress and aging: Possible role of neurotrophic factors. *Behavioral Brain Research,* 78(1):25–36.

Smith, M. A., S. Y. Kim, H. J. Van Oers, and S. Levine. 1997. Maternal deprivation and stress induce immediate early genes in the infant rat brain. *Endocrinology,* 138:4622–28.

Soubrie, P. 1986. Reconciling the role of central serotonin neurons in human and animal behavior. *The Behavioral and Brain Sciences,* 9:319–65.

Spivak, H., D. Prothrow-Stith, and A. J. Hausman. 1988. Dying is no accident. Adolescents, violence, and intentional injury. *Pediatric Clinics of North America,* 35(6):1339–47.

Spodak, M. K., Z. A. Falck, and J. R. Rappeport. 1978. The hormonal treatment of paraphiliacs with Depo-Provera. *Criminal Justice and Behavior,* 5:304–14.

Stabenau, J. R. 1977. Genetic and other factors in schizophrenic, manic-depressive, and schizo-affective psychoses. *Journal of Nervous and Mental Disorders,* 164(3):149–67.

Stein, M. B., C. Koverola, C. Hanna, M. G. Torchia, and B. McClarty. 1997b. Hippocampal volume in women victimized by childhood sexual abuse. *Psychological Medicine,* 27(4):951–59.

Stein, M. B., R. Yehuda, C. Koverola, and R. Hanna. 1997a. Enhanced dexamethasone suppression of plasma cortisol in adult women traumatized by childhood sexual abuse. *Biological Psychiatry,* 42:680–86.

Stokes, P. E. 1995. The potential role of excessive cortisol induced by HPA hyperfunction in the pathogenesis of depression. *European Neuropsychopharmacology,* 5 Suppl:77–82.

Streissguth, A. P., J. M. Aase, S. K. Clarren, S. P. Randels, R. A. LaDue, and D. F. Smith. 1991. Fetal alcohol syndrome in adolescents and adults. *Journal of the American Medical Association,* 265:1961–67.

Syndulko, D., D. A. Parker, R. Jens, I. Maltzman, and E. Ziskind. 1975. Psychophysiology of sociopathy: Electrocortical measures. *Biological Psychiatry,* 3:185–200.

Susman, E. J., L. D. Dorn, and G. P. Chrousos. 1991. Negative affect and hormone levels in young adolescents: Concurrent and predictive perspectives. *Journal of Youth and Adolescence,* 20:167–90.

Susman, E. J., and A. Ponirakis. 1997. Hormones—Context interactions and antisocial behavior in youth. In A. Raine, P. A. Brennan, D. P. Farrington, and S. A. Mednick (eds.), *Biosocial bases of violence.* New York: Plenum Press.

Tajuddin, N., and J. J. Druse. 1988. Chronic maternal ethanol consumption results in decreased serotonergic 5-HT1 sites in cerebral cortical regions from offspring. *Alcohol,* 5:465–70.

Tarter, R., and M. Vanyukov. 1994. Alcoholism: A developmental disorder. American Psychological Association. *Journal of Consulting and Clinical Psychology,* 62:1096–1107.

Tarter, R. E., H. Moss, T. Blackson, M. Vanyukov, J. Brigham, and R. Loeber. 1998. Disaggregating the liability for drug abuse. *NIDA Research Monograph,* 169:227–43.

Teicher, M. H., Y. Ito, C. A. Glod, S. L. Andersen, N. Dumont, and E. Ackerman. 1997. Preliminary evidence for abnormal cortical development in physically and sexually abused children using EEG coherence and MRI. *Annals of the New York Academy of Sciences,* 821:160–75.

Tennes, K., and M. Kreye. 1985. Children's adrenocortical response to classroom activities in elementary school. *Psychosomatic Medicine,* 47:451–60.

Tibbetts, S. G., and A. R. Piquero. 1999. The influence of gender, low birth weight, and disadvantaged environment in predicting early onset of offending: A test of Moffitt's interactional hypothesis. *Criminology,* forthcoming.

Tibbetts, S., and A. Piquero. 1999. The influence of gender, low birth weight, and disadvantaged environment in predicting early onset offending: a test of Moffitt's interactional hypothesis. *Criminology,* 37:843–878

Tiihonen, J., J. Kuikka, P. Hakola, J. Paanila, J. Airaksinen, M. Eronen, and T. Hallikainen. 1995. Acute ethanol-induced changes in cerebral blood flow. *American Journal of Psychiatry,* 151:1505–8.

Tsuang, M. T. 1983. Risk of suicide in relatives of schizophrenics, manic depressives and controls. *Journal of Clinical Psychiatry,* 44:396–400.

Uno, H., S. Eisele, A. Sakai, S. Shelton, E. Baker, O. DeJesus, and J. Holden. 1994. Neurotoxicity of glucocorticoids in the primate brain. *Hormones and Behavior,* 28:336–48.

van Goozen, S. H., P. T. Cohen-Kettenis, L. J. Gooren, H. H. Frijda, and N. E. Van de Poll. 1995. Gender differences in behaviour: Activating effects of cross-sex hormones. *Psychoneuroendocrinology,* 20:343–63.

van Goozen, S. H., W. Matthys, P. T. Cohen-Kettenis, J. H. Thijssen, and H. van Engeland. 1998. Adrenal androgens and aggression in conduct disorder prepubertal boys and normal controls. *Biological Psychiatry,* 43:156–58.

van Os, J., and J. P. Selten. 1998. Prenatal exposure to maternal stress and subsequent schizophrenia. The May 1940 invasion of The Netherlands. *British Journal of Psychiatry,* 172:324–26.

van Praag, H. M., R. S. Kahn, G. M. Asnis, S. Wetzler, S. L. Brown, A. Bleich, and M. L. Korn. 1987. Denosologization of biological psychiatry or the specificity of 5-HT disturbances in psychiatric disorders. *Journal of Affective Disorders,* 13:1–8.

Vila, B. 1997. Human nature and crime control: Improving the feasibility of nurturant strategies. *Politics and the Life Sciences,* 16:3–21.

Vila, B. J. 1994. A general paradigm for understanding criminal behavior: Extending evolutionary ecological theory. *Criminology,* 32:311–59.

Vila, B. J., and L. E. Cohen. 1993. Crime as strategy: Testing an evolutionary ecological theory of expropriative crime. *American Journal of Sociology,* 98:873–912.

Virgin, C. E., Jr., and R. M. Sapolsky. 1997. Styles of male social behavior and their endocrine correlates among low-ranking baboons. *American Journal of Primatology,* 42(1):25–39.

Virkkunen, M. 1983. Serum cholesterol levels in homicidal offenders: A low cholesterol level is connected with a habitually violent tendency under the influence of alcohol. *Psychophysiology,* 10:65–69.

———. 1984. Urinary free cortisol excretion in habitually violent offenders. *Acta Psychiatrica Scandinavica,* 72:40–42.

————. 1985. Urinary free cortisol secretion in habitually violent offenders. *Acta Psychiatrica Scandanavia,* 72(1):40–44.

Virkkunen, M., D. Goldman, and M. Linnoila. 1996. Serotonin in alcoholic violent offenders. Ciba Foundation Symposium, 194:168–77; discussion 177–82.

Virkkunen, M., E. Kallio, R. Rawlings, R. Tokola, R. E. Poland, A. Guidotti, C. Nemeroff, G. Bissette, K. Kalogeras, S. Karonen, and M. Linnoila. 1994a. Personality profiles and state aggressiveness in Finnish alcoholic, violent offenders, fire starters, and healthy volunteers. *Archives of General Psychiatry,* 51:28–33.

Virkkunen, M., and M. Linnoila. 1990. Serotonin in early onset, male alcoholics with violent behaviour. *Annals of Medicine,* 22:327–331.

————. 1993. Serotonin in personality disorders with habitual violence and impulsivity. In S. Hodgins (ed.), *Mental disorder and crime* (pp. 227–43). Newbury Park, CA: Sage.

Virkkunen, M., A. Nuutila, F. K. Goodwin, and M. Linnoila. 1987. Cerebrospinal fluid monoamine metabolite levels in male arsonists. *Archives of General Psychiatry,* 44:241–47.

————. 1989. Relationship of psychobiological variables to recidivism in violent offenders and impulsive fire setters. *Archives of General Psychiatry,* 46:600–603.

Virkkunen, M., R. Rawlings, R. Tokola, R. E. Poland, A. Guidotti, C. Nemeroff, G. Bissette, K. Kalogeras, S. Karonen, and M. Linnoila. 1994b. CSF biochemistries, glucose metabolism, and diurnal activity rhythms in alcoholic, violent offenders, fire setters, and healthy volunteers. *Archives of General Psychiatry,* 51:20–27.

Volavka, J. 1995. *Neurobiology of violence.* Washington, D.C.: American Psychiatric Press.

von Knorring, L., A-L. von Knorring, L. Smigan, U. Lindberg, and M. Edholm. 1987. Personality traits in subtypes of alcoholics. *Journal of Studies on Alcohol,* 48:523–27.

Voss, L. D., J. Mulligan, and P. R. Betts. 1998. Short stature at school entry—an index of social deprivation? (The Wessex Growth Study). *Child Care and Health Development,* 24:145–56.

Wakschlag, L. S., B. B. Lahey, R. Loeber, S. M. Green, J. R. A. Gordon, and B. L. Leventhal. 1997. Maternal smoking during pregnancy and the risk of conduct disorder in boys. *Archives of General Psychiatry,* 54(7):670–76.

Waldrop, M. F., and C. F. Halverson, Jr. 1971. Minor Physical Anomalies. In *Exceptional infant,* J. Hellmuth (ed.). New York: Brunner/Mazel.

Wallace, D. M., D. J. Magnuson, and T. S. Gray. 1992. Organization of amygdaloid projections to brainstem dopaminergic, noradrenergic, and adrenergic cell groups in the rat. *Brain Research Bulletin,* 27:447–54.

Ward, A. J. 1991. Prenatal stress and childhood psychopathology. *Child Psychiatry and Human Development,* 22:97–110.

Wenk E. A., J. O. Robison, and G. W. Smith. 1972. Can violence be predicted? *Crime and Delinquency,* 18:393–402.

Wilson, E. O. 1998. *Consilience.* San Francisco, CA: Knopf.

Wilson, J. Q., and R. Hernnstein. 1985. *Crime and human nature.* New York: Simon & Schuster.

Woodman, D. 1979. Evidence of a permanent imbalance in catecholamine secretion in violent social deviants. *Journal of Psychosomatic Research,* 23:155–57.

Woodman, D., and J. Hinton. 1978. Catecholamine balance during stress anticipation: Abnormalities in maximum security hospital patients. *Journal of Psychosomatic Research,* 22:477–83.

Woodman, D., J. Hinton, and M. O'Neill. 1977. Relationship between violence and catecholamines. *Perceptual and Motor Skills,* 45:702.

Yamamoto, K., H. Arai, and S. Nakayama. 1990. Skin conductance response after 6-hydroxy-dopamine lesion of central noradrenaline system in cats. *Biological Psychiatry*, 28:151–60.

Zametkin, A. J., T. E. Nordahl, M. Gross, A. C. King, W. E. Semple, J. Rumsey, S. Hamburger, and R. M. Cohen. 1990. Cerebral glucose metabolism in adults with hyperactivity of childhood onset. *New England Journal of Medicine*, 323:1361–66.

Zuckerman B., and K. Bresnahan. 1991. Developmental and behavioral consequences of prenatal drug and alcohol exposure. *Pediatric Clinics of North America*, 38(6):1387–406.

Credits

fig. 4–7, p. 54 (photo) Richard Nowitz/Corbis

fig. 4–8, p. 56 "The Prefrontal Cortex," by J. M. Fuster, 1989. Copyright 1989 Raven Press. Reprinted by permission.

fig. 4–9, p. 58 American Association for the Advancement of Science. Reprinted with permission from "The Return of Phineas Gage: Clues about the Brain From the Skull of a Famous Patient," by H. Damasio, T. Grabowski, R. Frank, A. M. Galabu, and A. R. Damasio in Science, 264. Photo © 1994.

fig. 6–1, p. 89 from "Cocaine-Induced Reduction of Glucose Utilization in Human Brain" by E. D. London et al, Archives of General Psychiatry, 1990, 47:567-74. Copyright 1990, American Medical Association. Used by permission of the AMA and E. D. London.

Index